Other humor books available from InterVarsity Press:

Amusing Grace by Ed Koehler
As the Church Turns by Ed Koehler
Church Is Stranger Than Fiction by Mary Chambers
Climbing the Church Walls by Rob Portlock
It Came from Beneath the Pew by Rob Suggs
Less Than Entirely Sanctified by Doug Hall
Murphy Goes to Church by Steve Dennie and Rob Suggs
Off the Church Wall by Rob Portlock
The Potluck Hall of Fame by David Dickerson and Mary Chambers
Preacher from the Black Lagoon by Rob Suggs
Way Off the Church Wall by Rob Portlock

REBORN TO BE Wild!

Doug Hall

InterVarsity Press
DOWNERS GROVE, ILLINOIS 60515

© *1993 by Doug Hall*

All rights reserved. No part of this book may be reproduced in any form without written permission from InterVarsity Press, P.O. Box 1400, Downers Grove, Illinois 60515.

InterVarsity Press is the book-publishing division of InterVarsity Christian Fellowship®, a student movement active on campus at hundreds of universities, colleges and schools of nursing in the United States of America, and a member movement of the International Fellowship of Evangelical Students. For information about local and regional activities, write Public Relations Dept., InterVarsity Christian Fellowship, 6400 Schroeder Rd., P.O. Box 7895, Madison, WI 53707-7895.

Cover illustration: Doug Hall

ISBN 0-8308-1838-3

Printed in the United States of America ∞

Library of Congress Cataloging-in-Publication Data

Hall, Doug, 1956-
    Reborn to be wild/Doug Hall.
      p.   cm.
    ISBN 0-8308-1838-3
    1. Churches—Caricatures and cartoons.   2. American wit and humor,
Pictorial.   I. Title.
NC1429.H323A4   1993b
741.5'973—dc20   93-19211
                                                  CIP

17	16	15	14	13	12	11	10	9	8	7	6	5	4	3	2	1
07	06	05	04	03	02	01	00	99	98	97	96	95	94	93		

*For Ken and Arlene,
beloved parents
and wild people of faith*

Introduction

In many ways, I am courage-impaired. I'm intimidated by crowds, large geese and gravelly voiced telephone salesmen who use the term "youse guys." When it comes to public speaking, not only would I "rather be sailing," I'd rather be having bypass surgery. I recently read that Woody Allen is afraid of drains which are located in the center of shower stall floors. I'm not subject to that particular fear at the moment, but I have it under study.

The problem is, timidity does not really mesh well with Christianity. God wants us to be free from pointless fears, and he has things for us to do that require a certain wild boldness. I'm working on that (and so are the characters in many of the following cartoons).

Fortunately, God has placed people in my life who have things to teach about courage. I have many friends and relatives who minister in hazardous parts of the globe, such as junior-high classrooms.

One of my current tutors in bravery is my two-year-old son, Jonathan. In spite of a limited vocabulary, Jonathan is unafraid to enthusiastically greet any creature or inanimate object within waving range. He is utterly oblivious to the day-to-day worries that soak up so much of my attention. He has a wild, powerful joy of the sort I believe Christians are reborn to possess.

Doug Hall

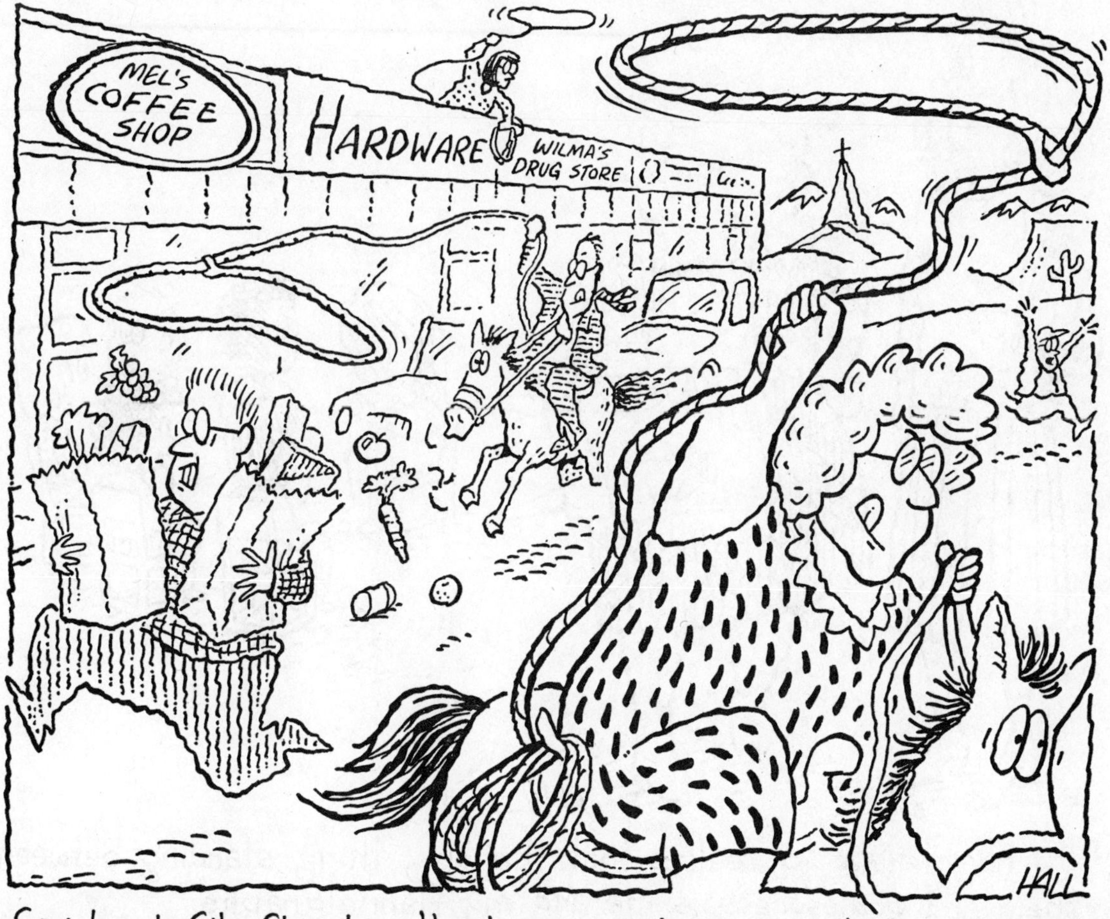
MEL'S COFFEE SHOP
HARDWARE
WILMA'S DRUG STORE
HALL

Initially, Sagebrush City Church's attendance round-up generated impressive numbers.

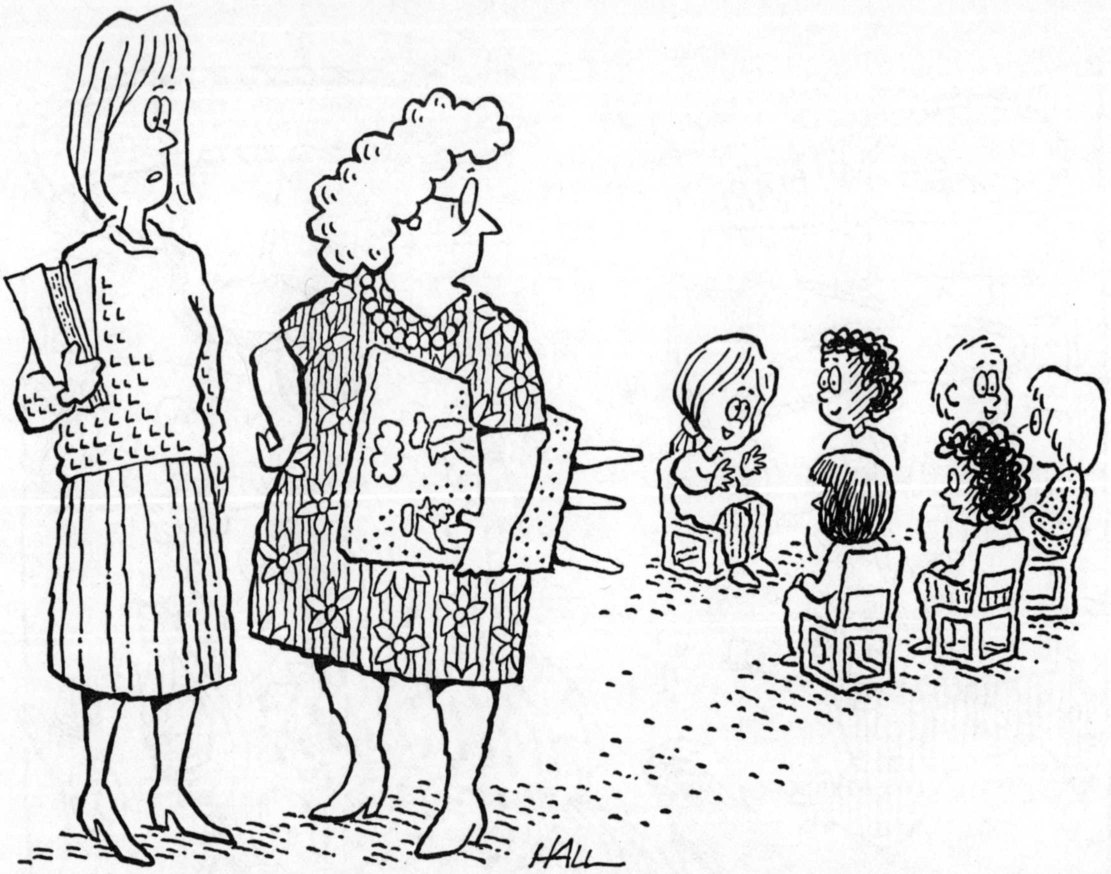
HALL

"It's frightening to realize that the only thing standing between them and godlessness is me and my flannelgraphs."

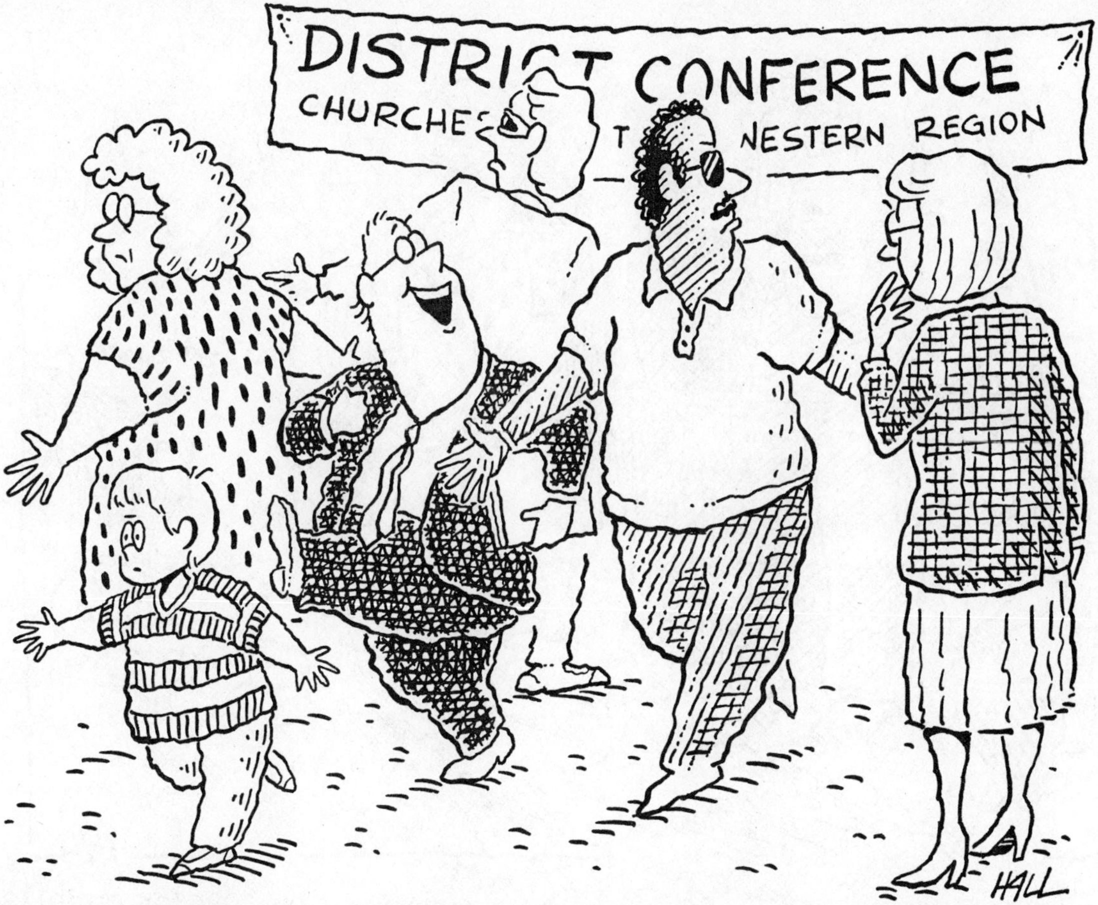
DISTRICT CONFERENCE
CHURCHES
T
WESTERN REGION
HALL

"My congregation is afraid some other church will try to steal me away."

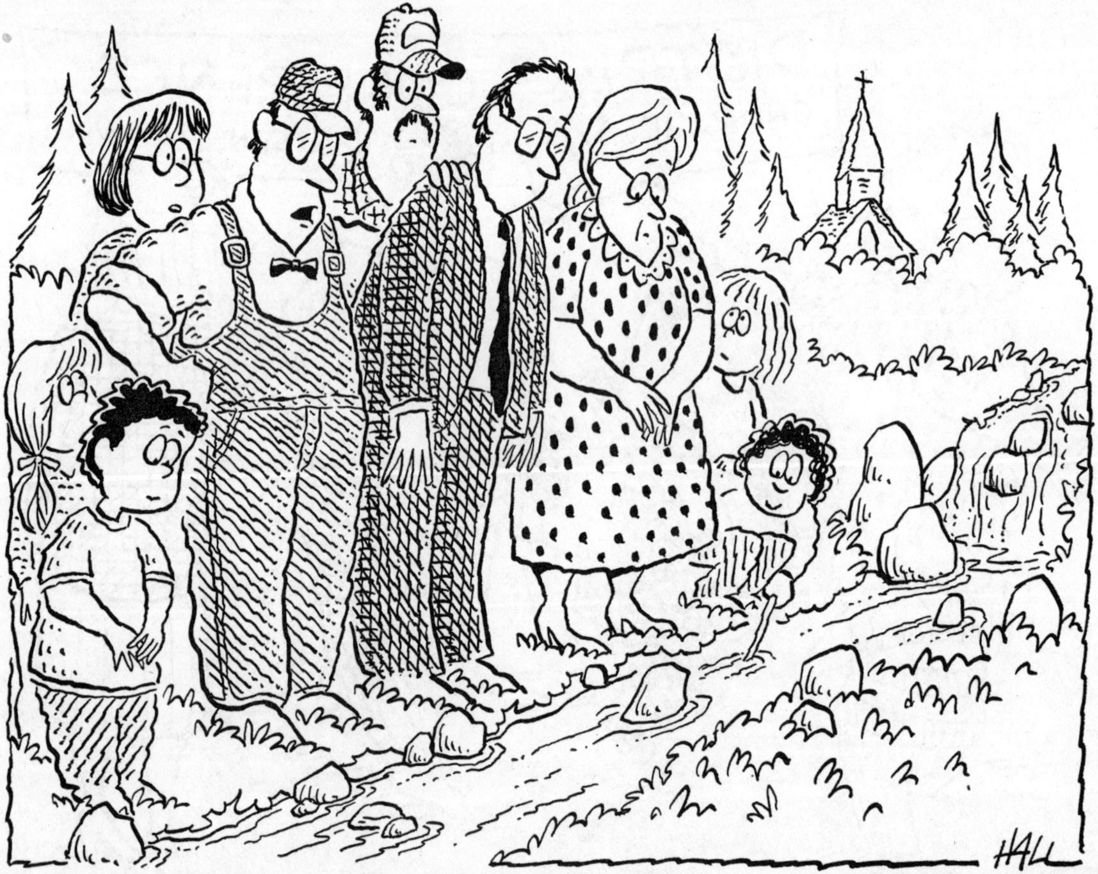
HALL

"If Moses could part the Red Sea, we figure our pastor oughtta be able to do <u>somethin'</u> with Muddy Branch Crick."

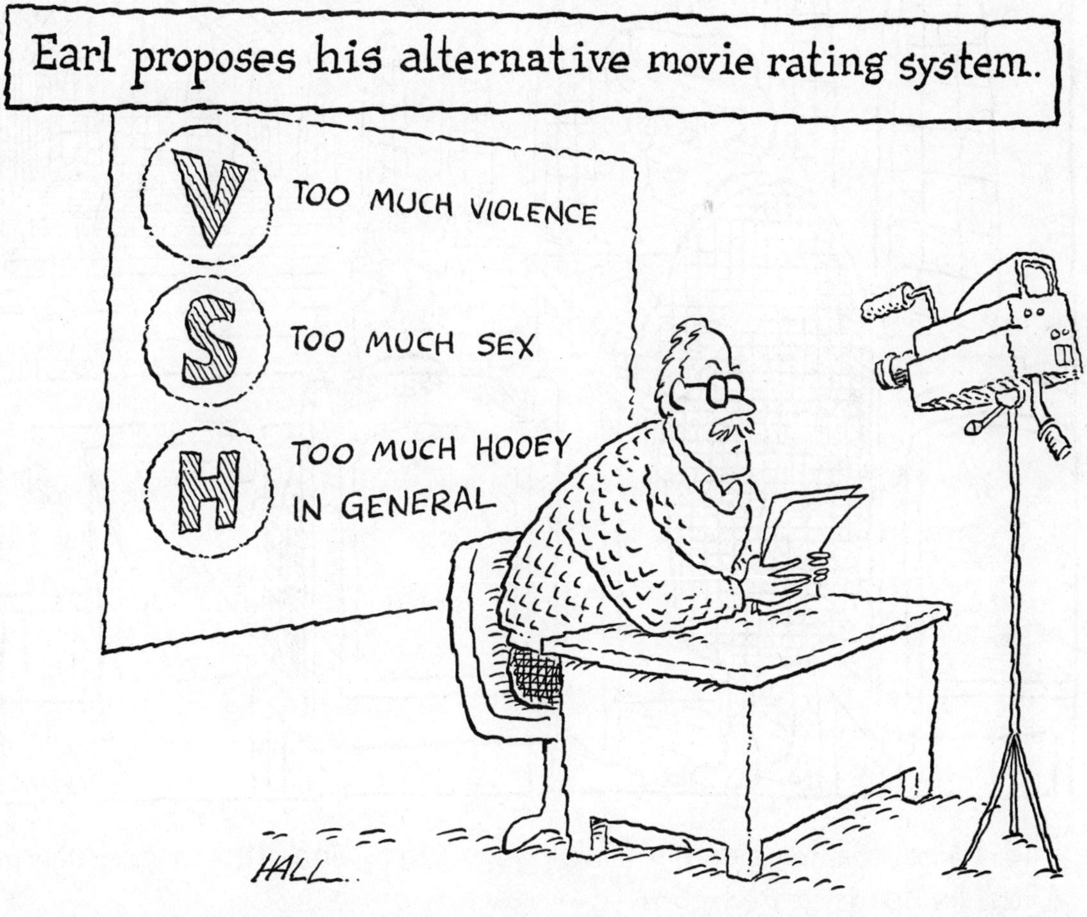
Earl proposes his alternative movie rating system.
V TOO MUCH VIOLENCE
S TOO MUCH SEX
H TOO MUCH HOOEY IN GENERAL
HALL

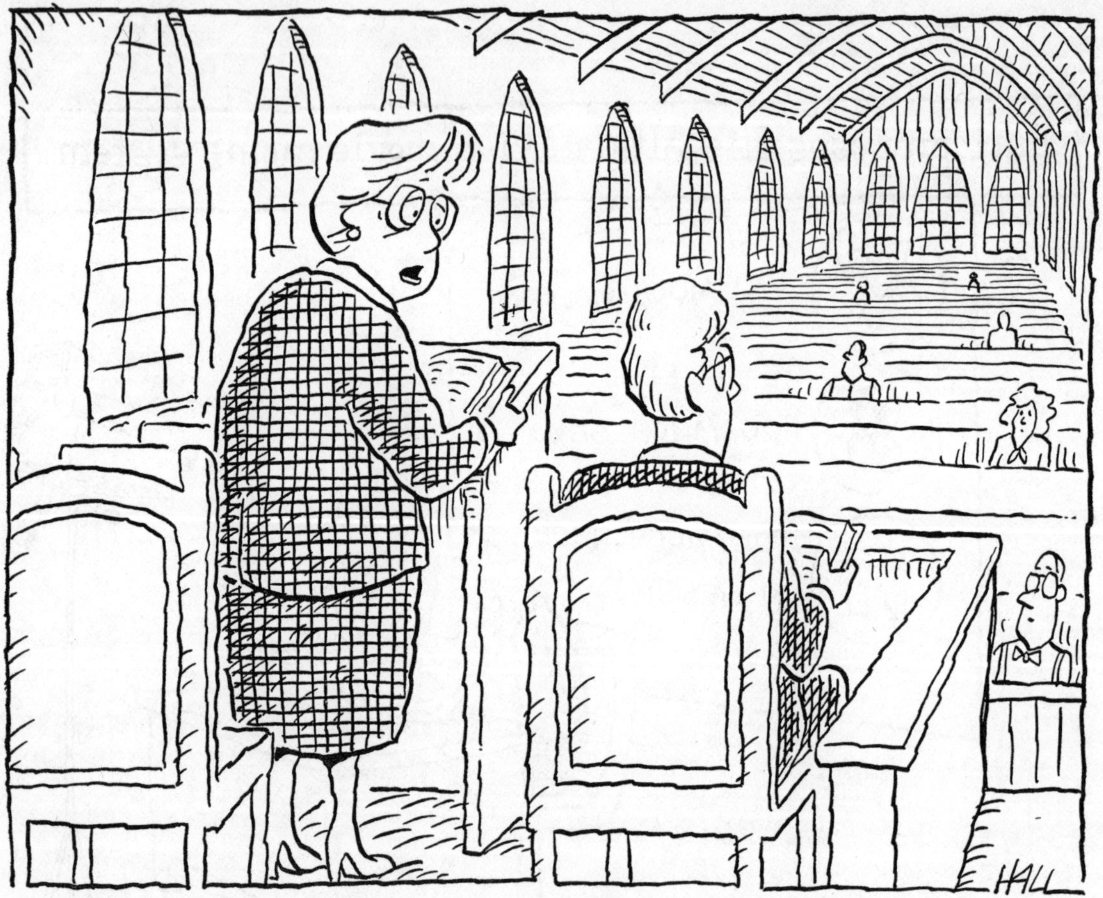
HALL

"The former pastor saw his ministry as winnowing the congregation down to its dedicated core."

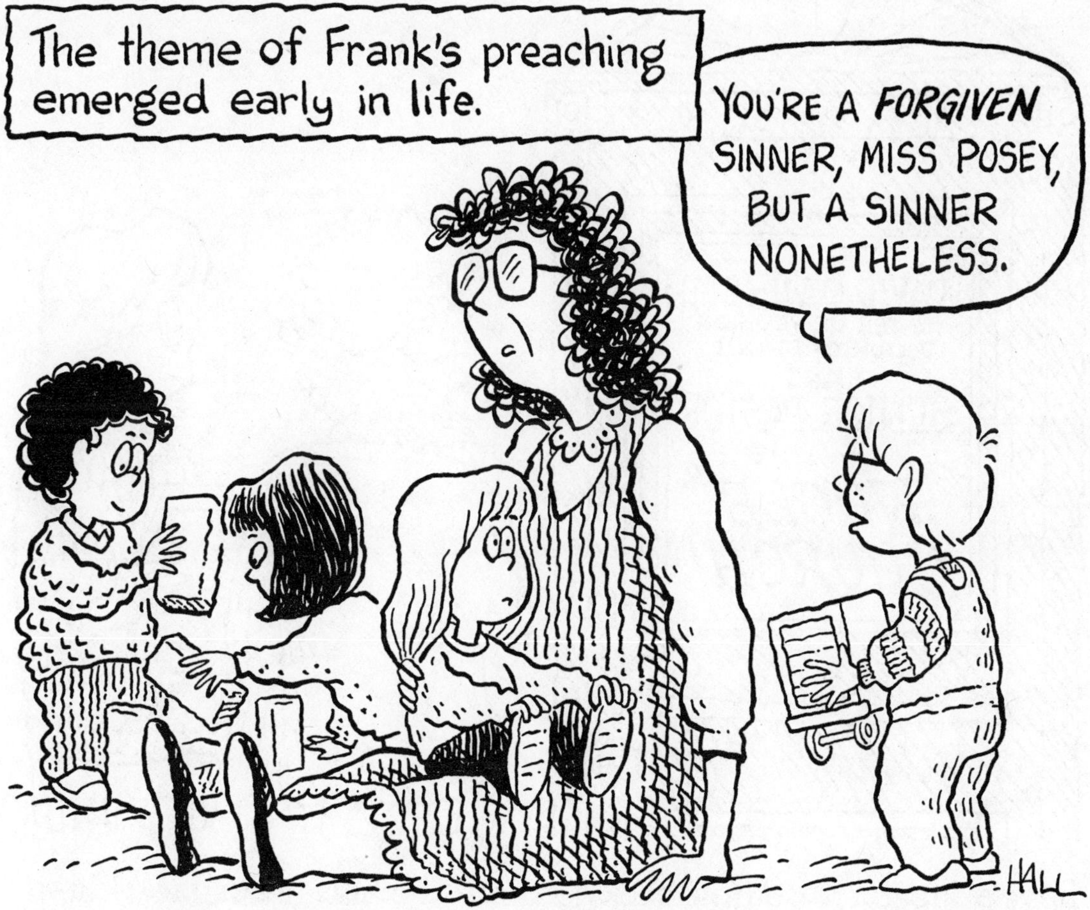
The theme of Frank's preaching emerged early in life.
YOU'RE A FORGIVEN SINNER, MISS POSEY, BUT A SINNER NONETHELESS.
HALL

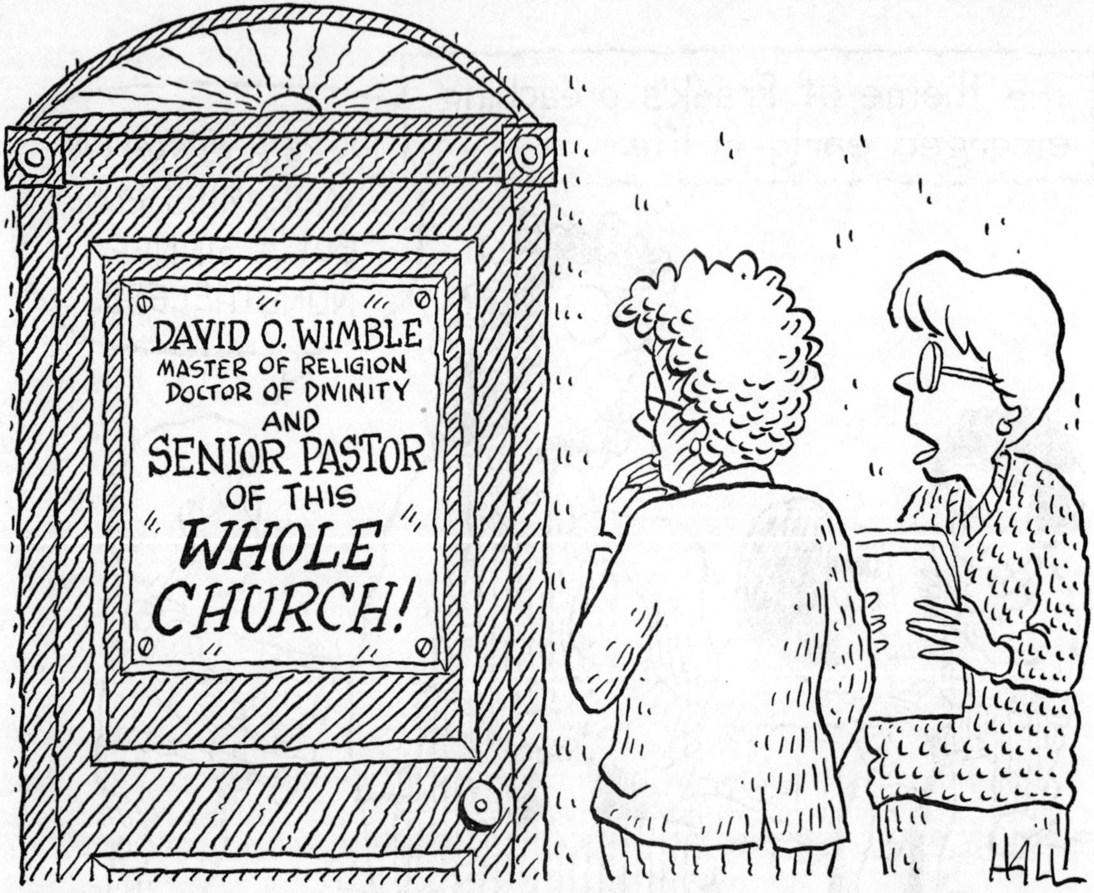
DAVID O. WIMBLE
MASTER OF RELIGION
DOCTOR OF DIVINITY
AND
SENIOR PASTOR
OF THIS
WHOLE
CHURCH!
HALL

"Dave's insecurity dates back to the time his seminary class voted him 'Least Likely to Grow Out of Youth Ministry.'"

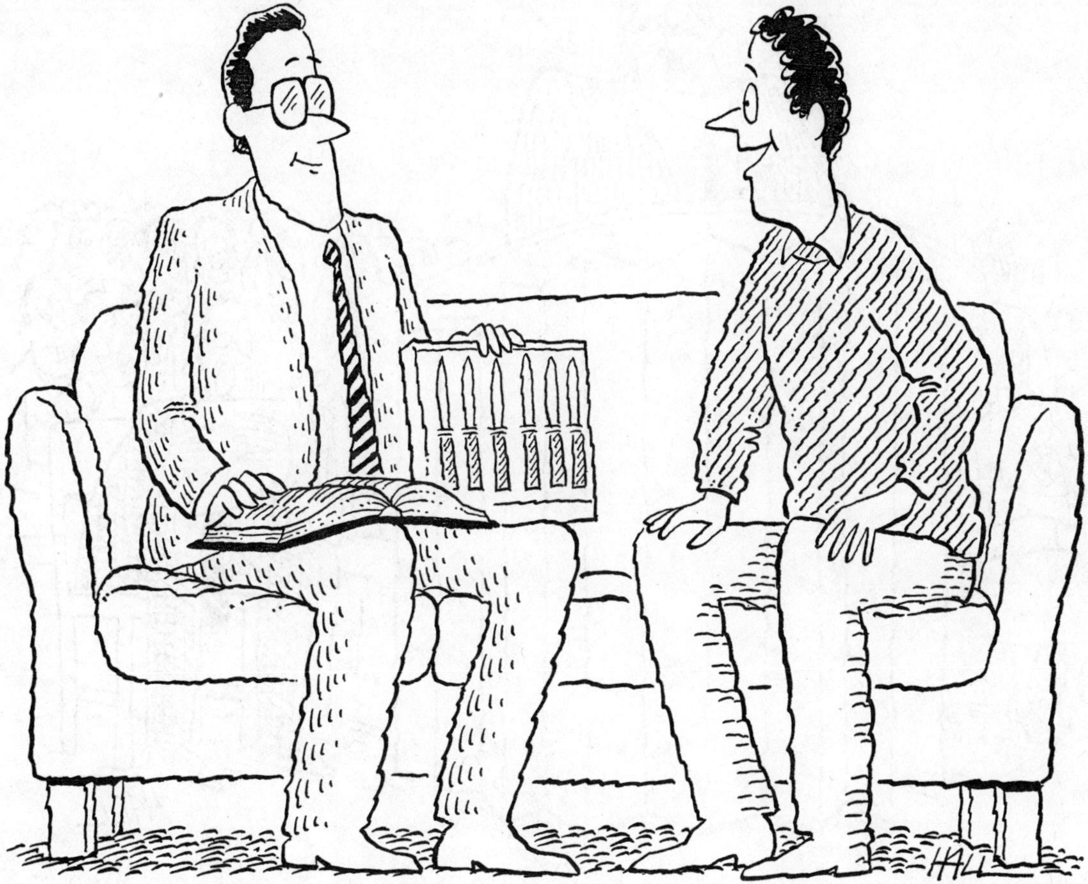
HALL

"Let me get this straight.... I'll inherit eternal life *and* get the free set of steak knives?"

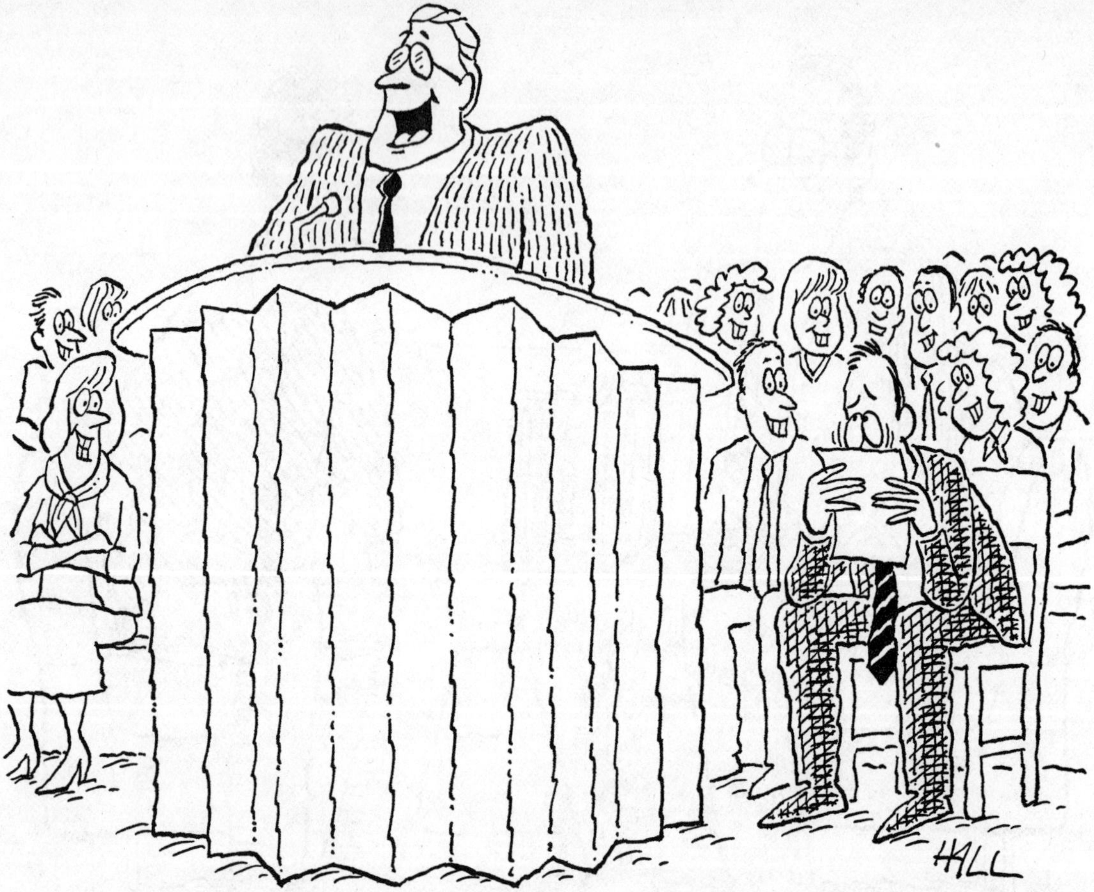
HALL

"I'm sure my good brother Jimmy Joe Keeters won't mind if I tell a little story on him..."

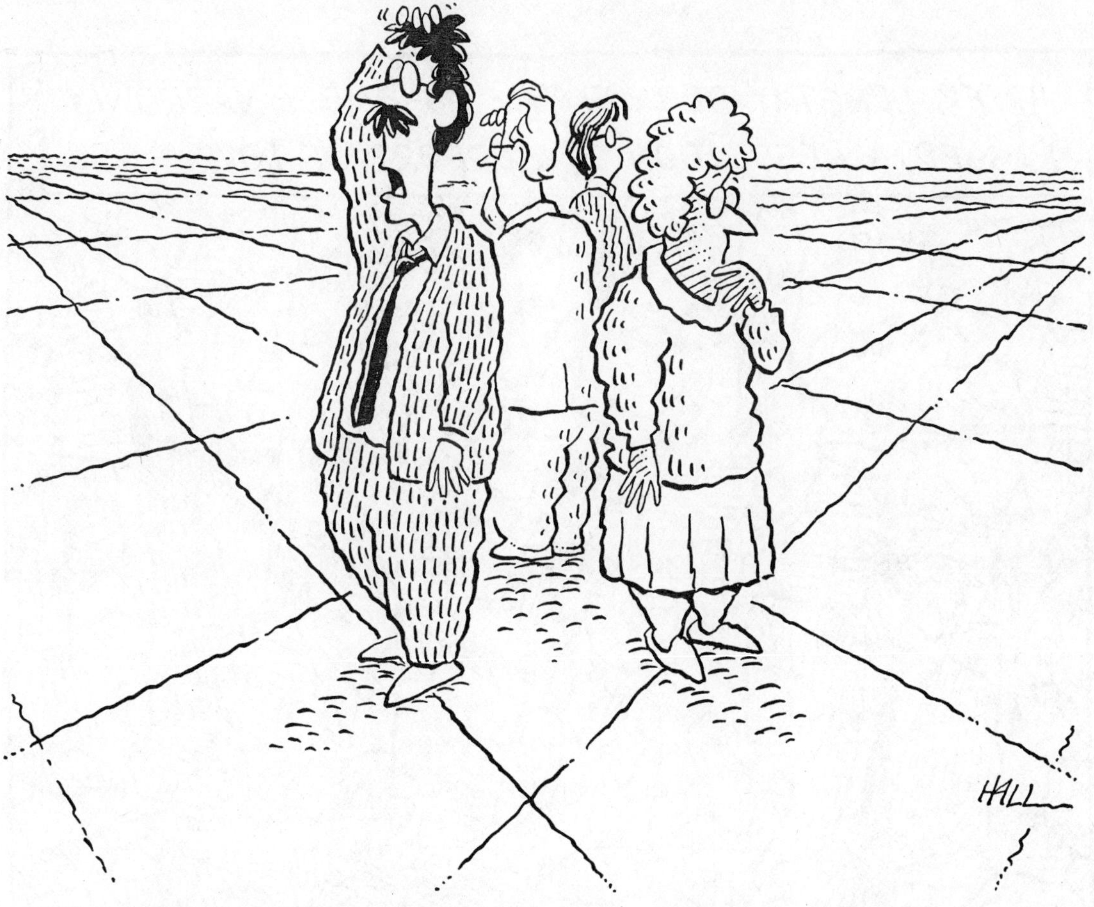
HALL

"Did anyone happen to bring a moral compass?"

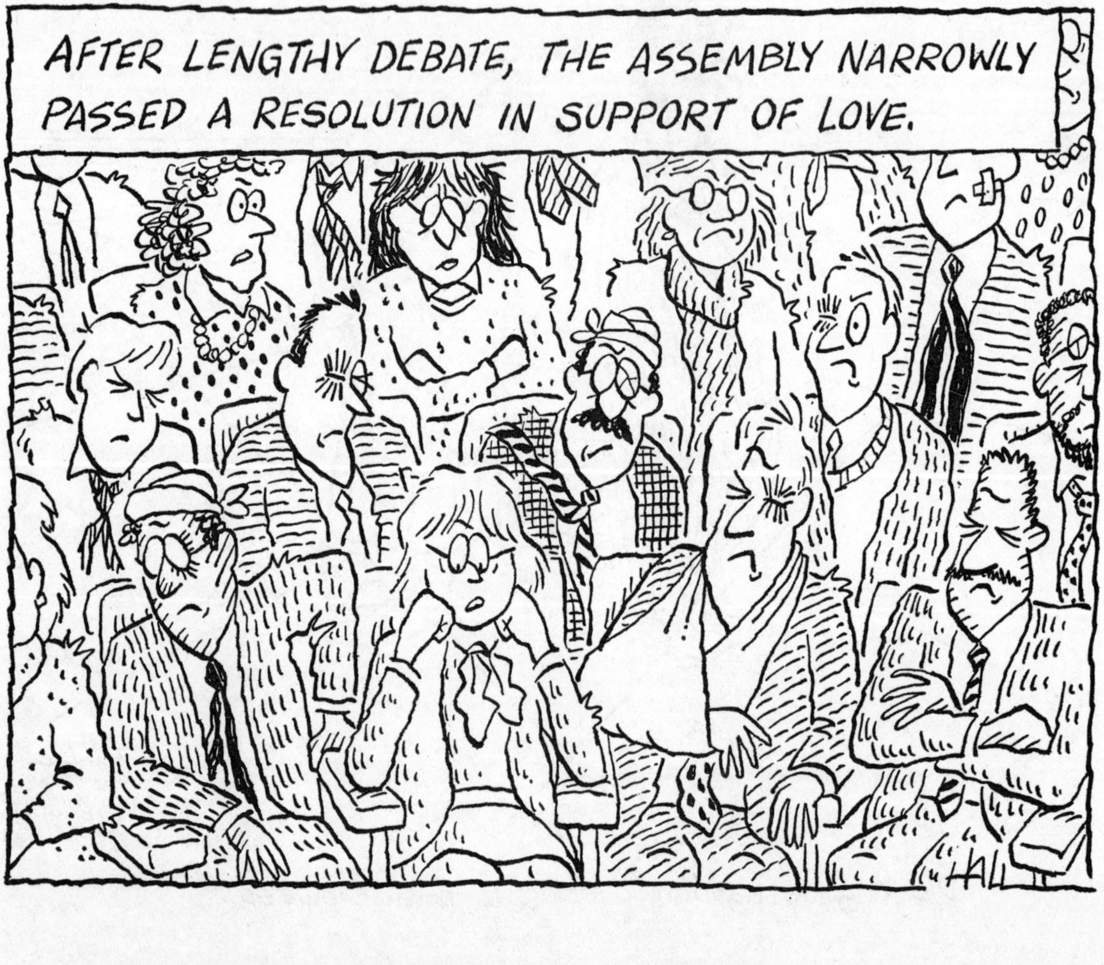
AFTER LENGTHY DEBATE, THE ASSEMBLY NARROWLY PASSED A RESOLUTION IN SUPPORT OF LOVE.
HALL

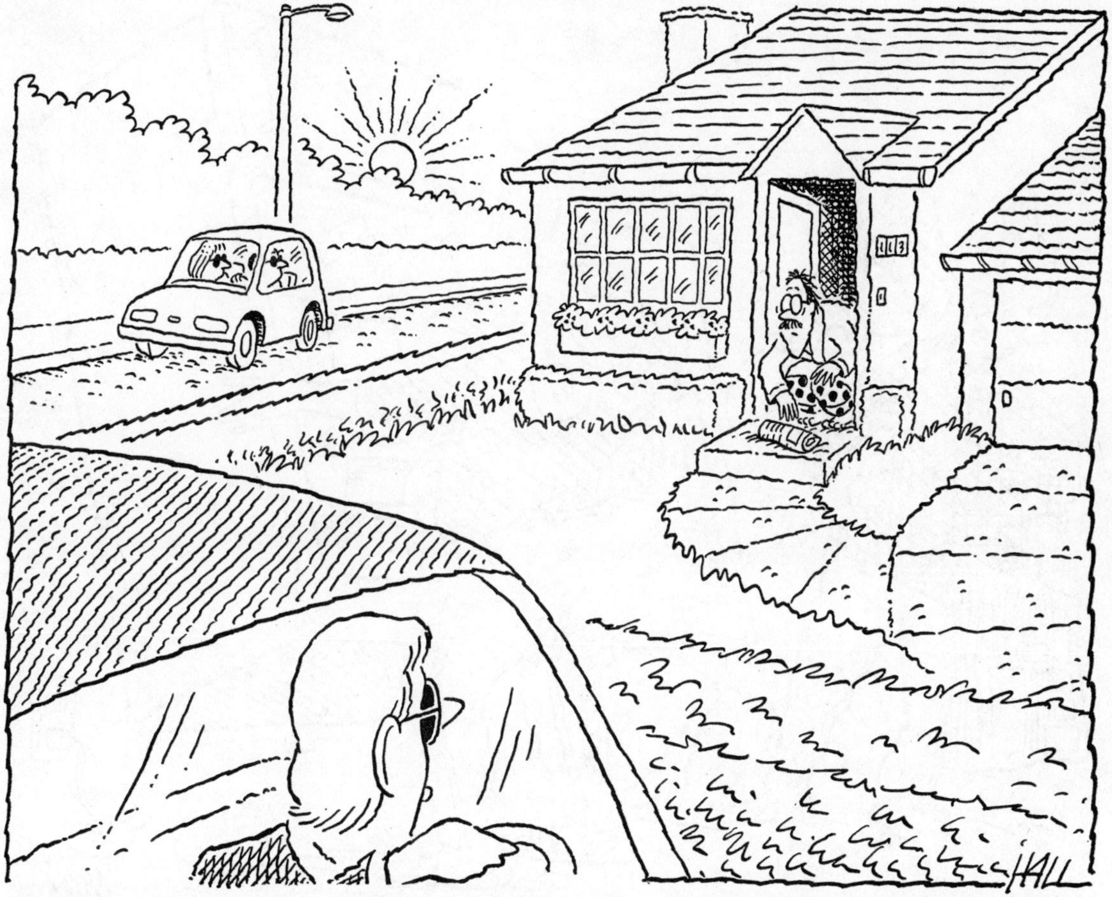
HALL

Sunday, 7:15 a.m. — The Welcoming Committee stakes out last week's first-time visitor.

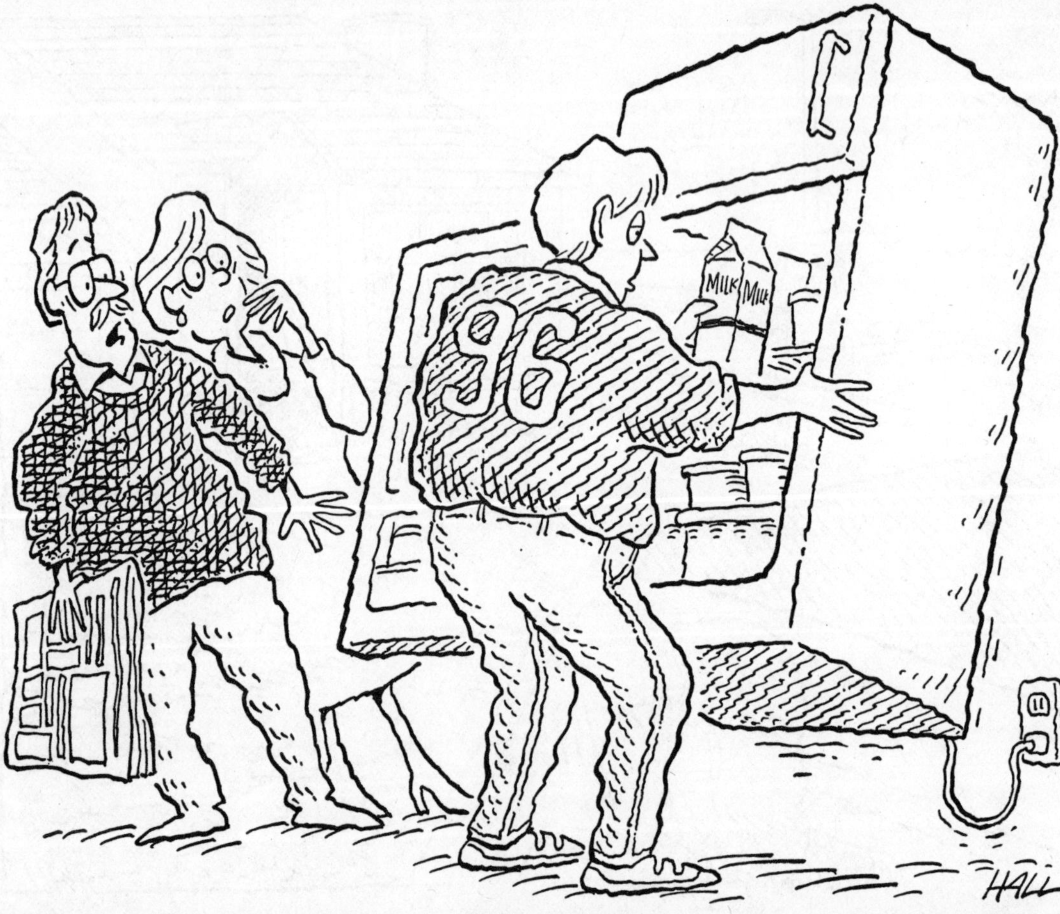
96
MILK
MILK
HALL

"As Jeffrey gets older, it takes more daring to discipline."

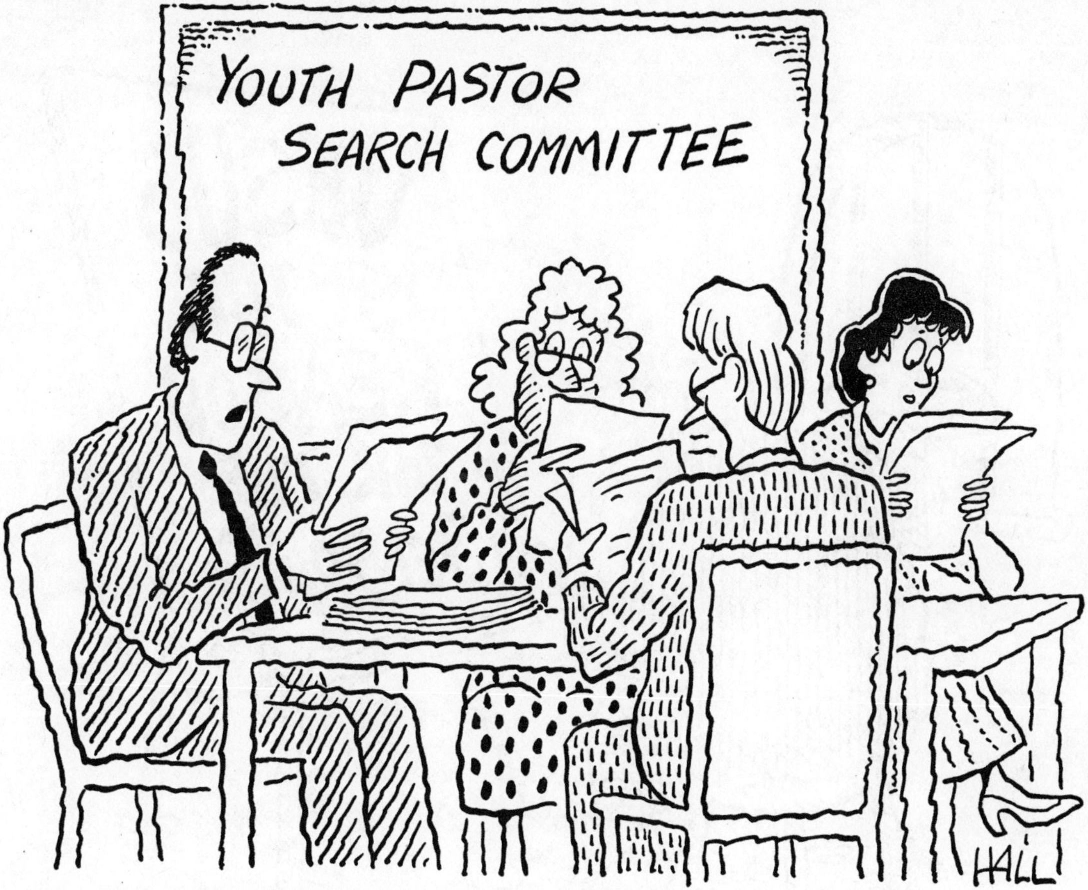
YOUTH PASTOR
SEARCH COMMITTEE
HALL

"This candidate is young and idealistic ... We ought to be able to shave about $5,000 off his starting salary."

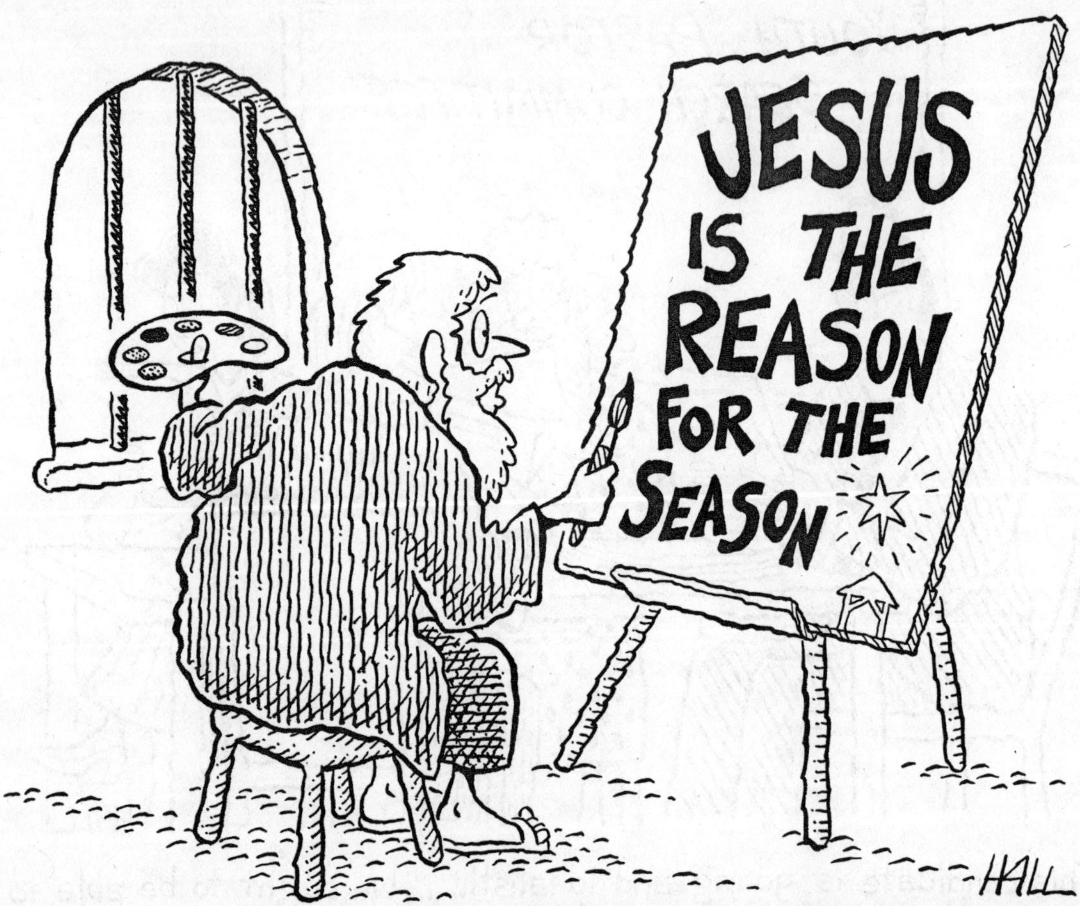
JESUS IS THE REASON FOR THE SEASON
HALL

As with his letters, the text of Paul's posters survived.

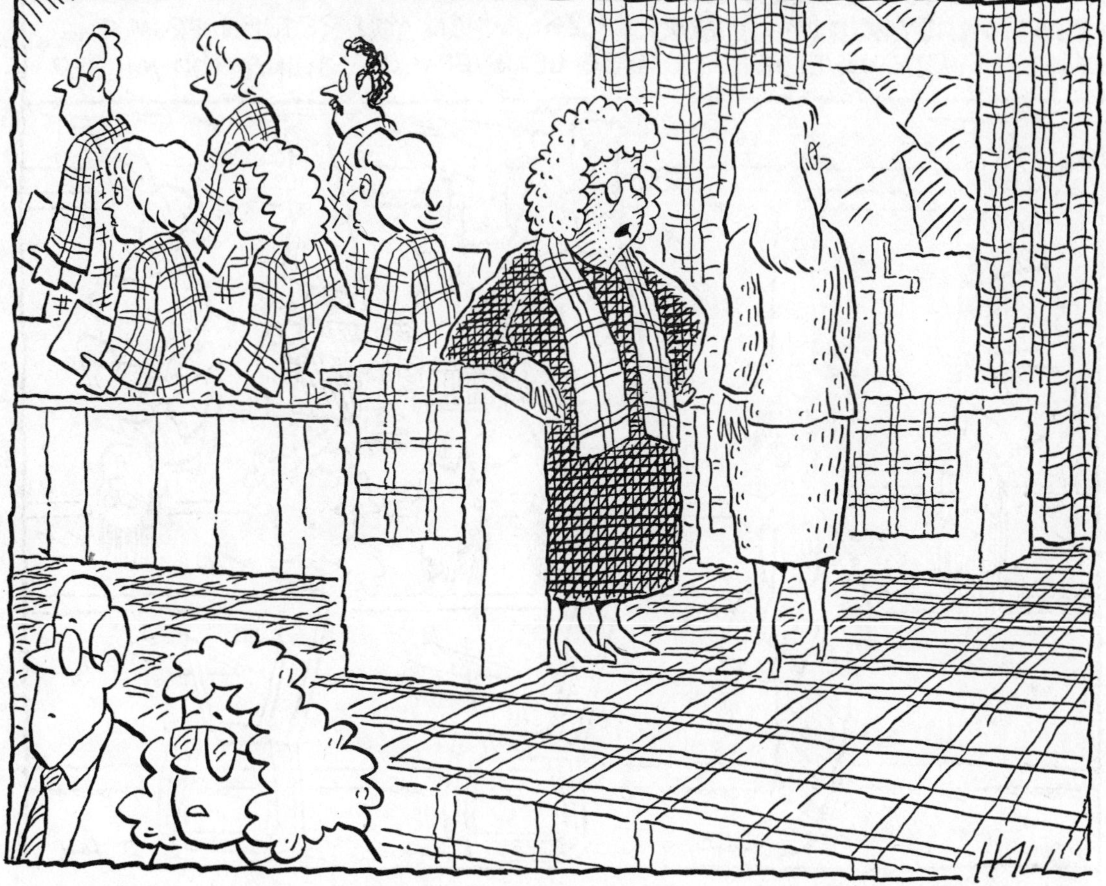
HALL

"The trustees found an incredible deal on the fabric."

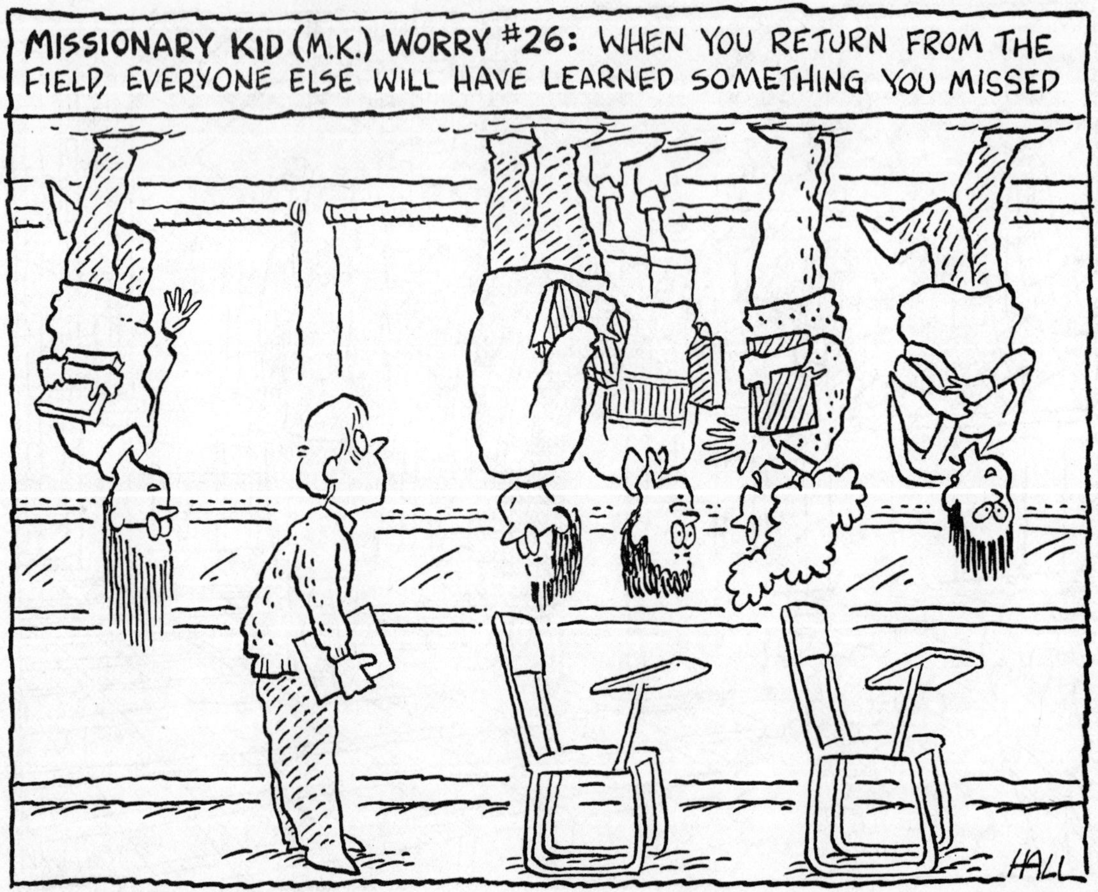
MISSIONARY KID (M.K.) WORRY #26: WHEN YOU RETURN FROM THE FIELD, EVERYONE ELSE WILL HAVE LEARNED SOMETHING YOU MISSED
HALL

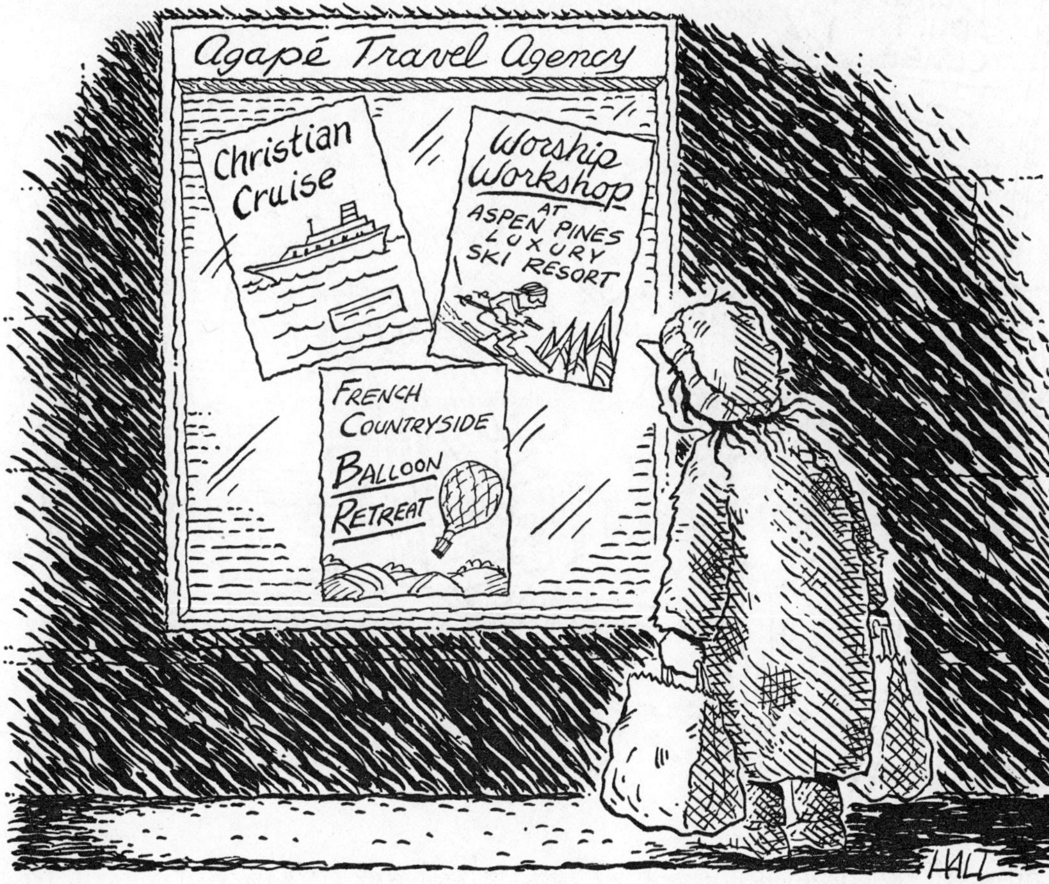

Agapé Travel Agency
Christian Cruise
Worship Workshop AT ASPEN PINES LUXURY SKI RESORT
FRENCH COUNTRYSIDE BALLOON RETREAT
HALL

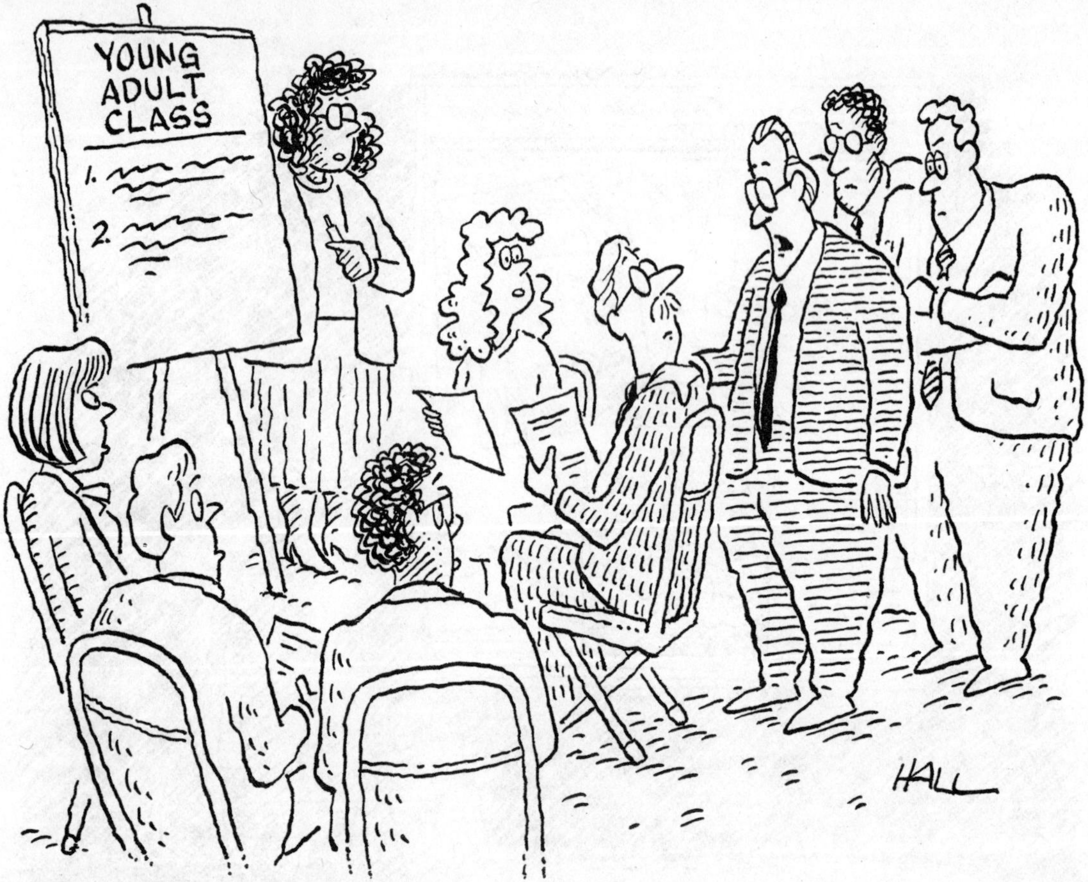
YOUNG
ADULT
CLASS
1.
2.
HALL

"Come along quietly, Carl. Your latest birthday puts you in with the Middle Agers."

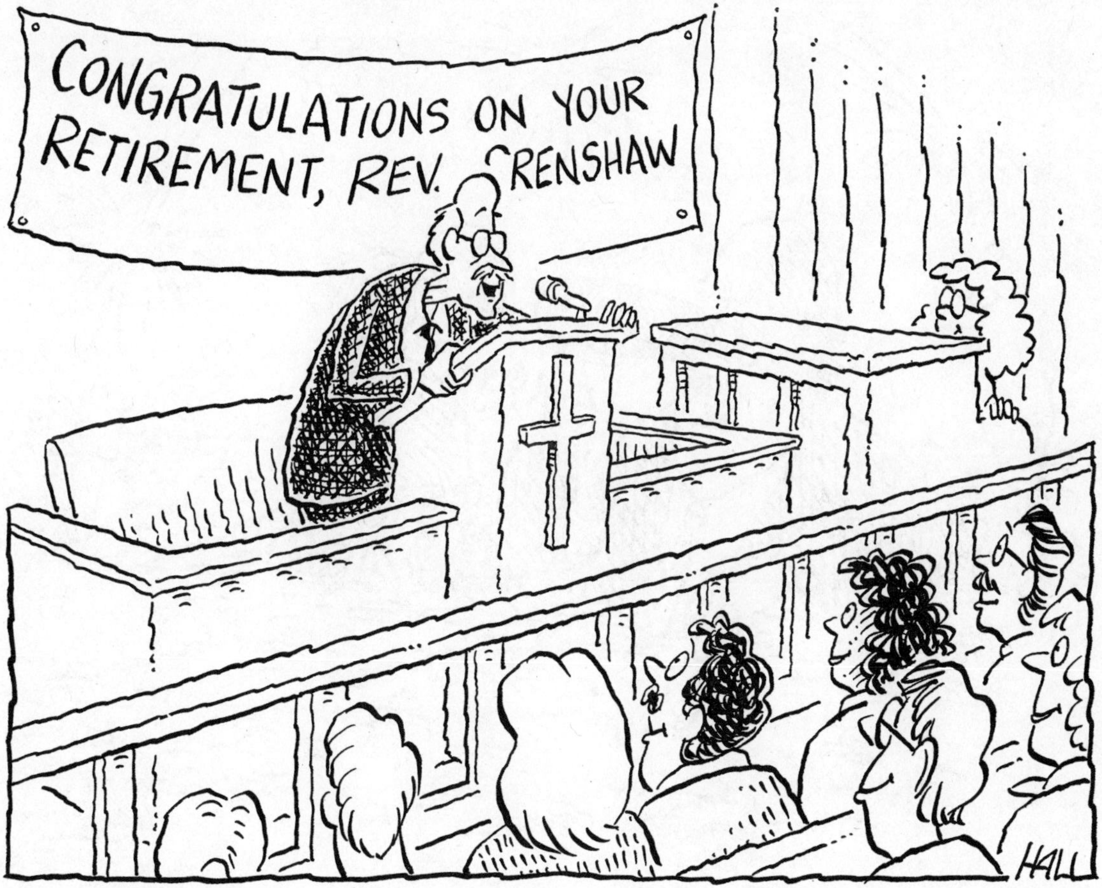
CONGRATULATIONS ON YOUR RETIREMENT, REV. CRENSHAW
HALL

"For 35 years, I've dedicated you, baptized you, prayed with you, married you, and buried you. It's been a real blast!"

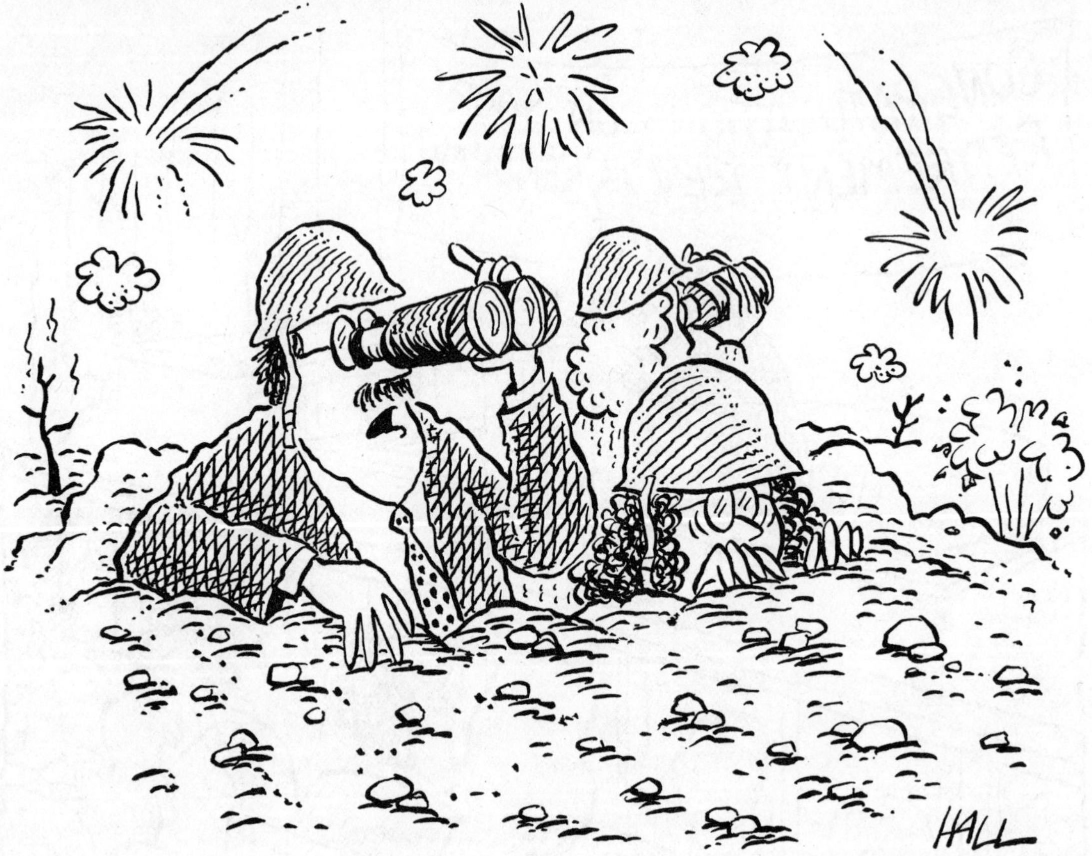
HALL

"Keep calm, Miss Fenstermeyer. They always told us the secular humanists would come for us someday."

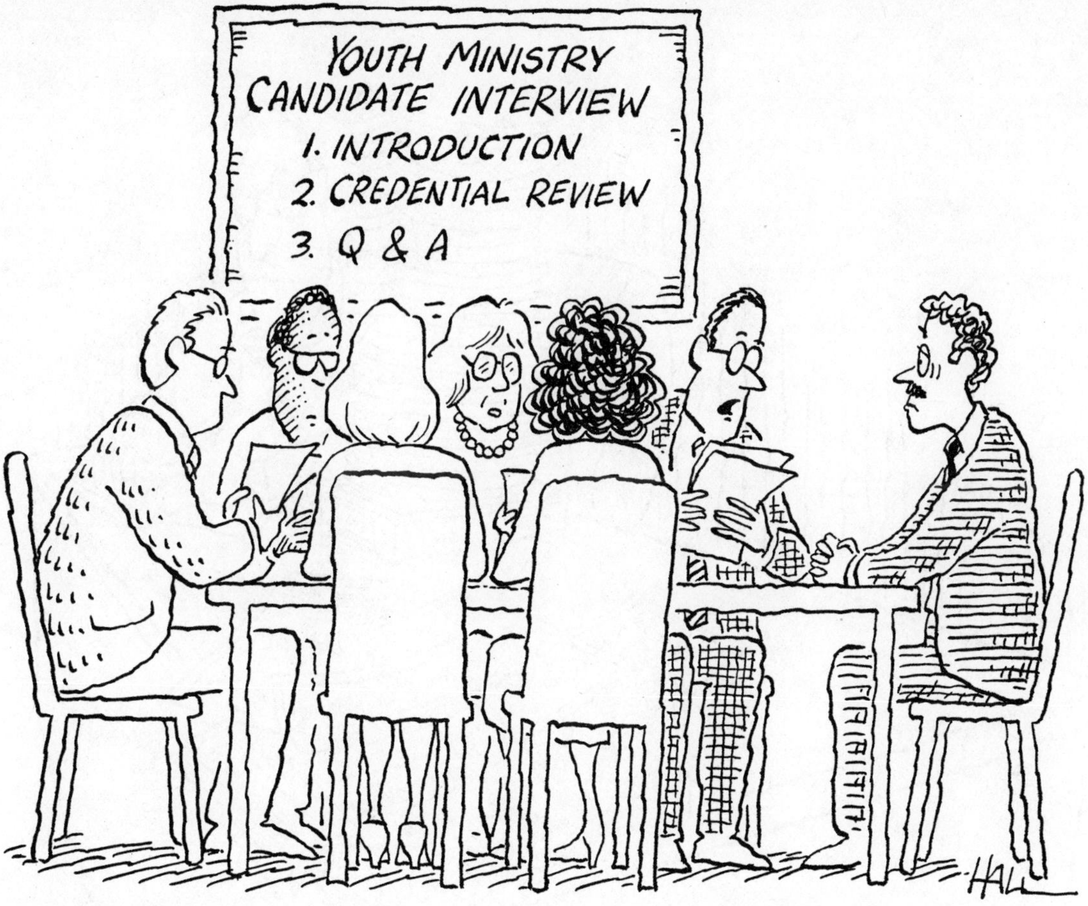
YOUTH MINISTRY
CANDIDATE INTERVIEW
1. INTRODUCTION
2. CREDENTIAL REVIEW
3. Q & A
HALL

"Don't be nervous, kid. We call a pastor, but we only hire a youth minister."

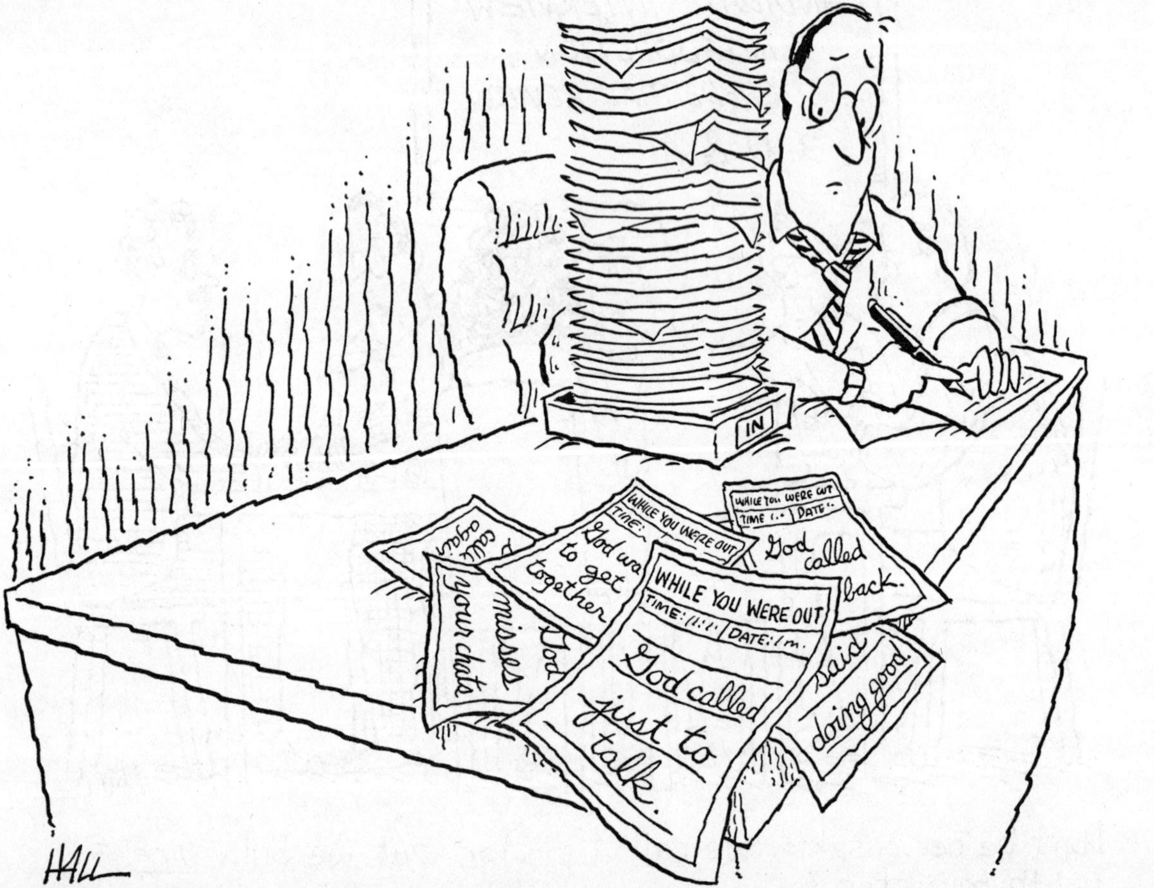

IN
WHILE YOU WERE OUT
TIME
DATE
God called back.
WHILE YOU WERE OUT
TIME:
to get together
God misses your chats
WHILE YOU WERE OUT
TIME:
DATE:
God called just to talk.
said doing good.
HALL

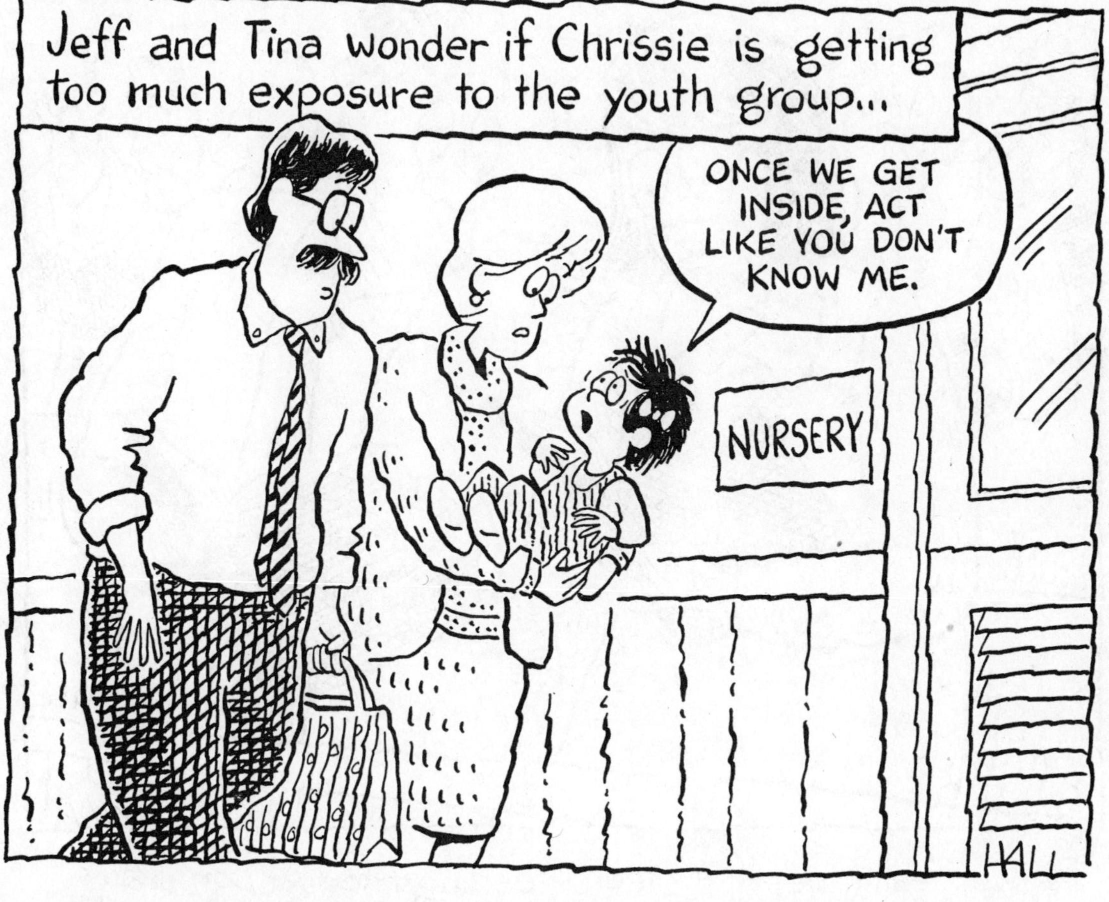
Jeff and Tina wonder if Chrissie is getting too much exposure to the youth group...
ONCE WE GET INSIDE, ACT LIKE YOU DON'T KNOW ME.
NURSERY
HALL

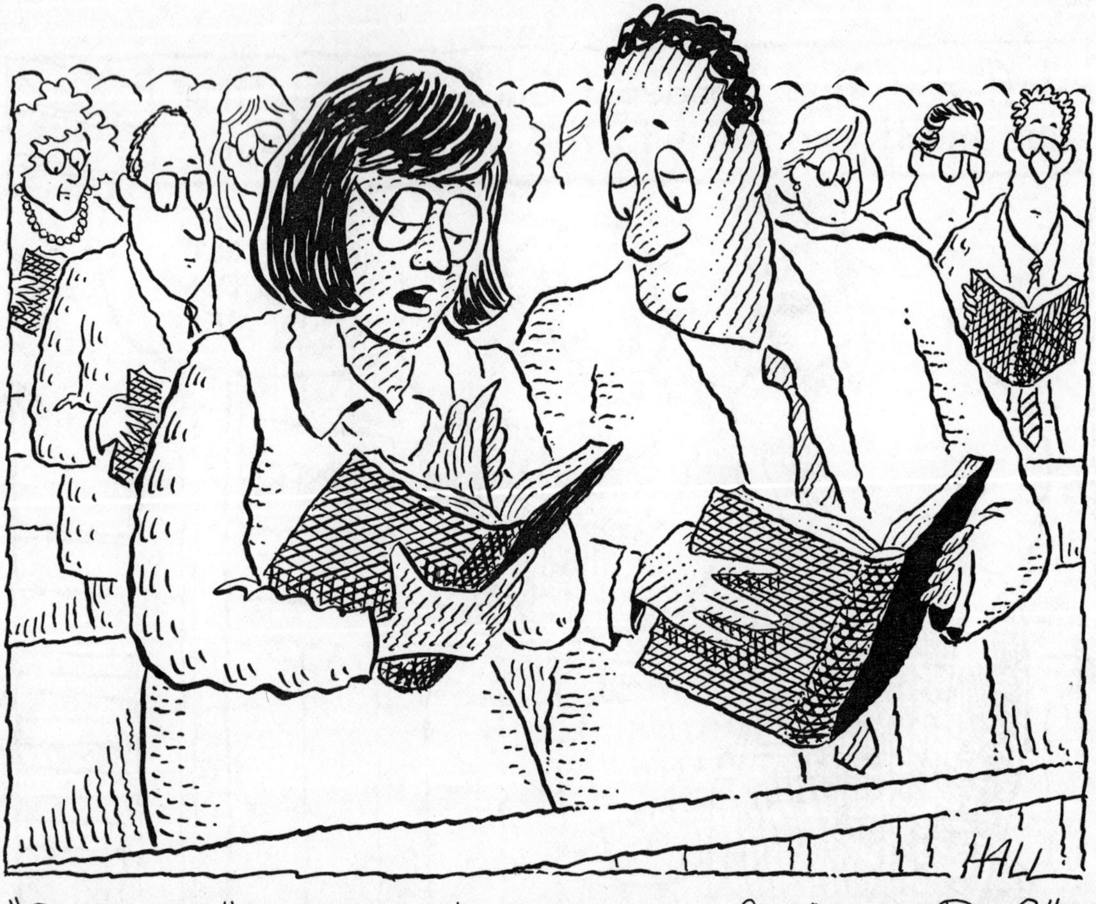
HALL

"Do we really need sixteen readings for Arbor Day?"

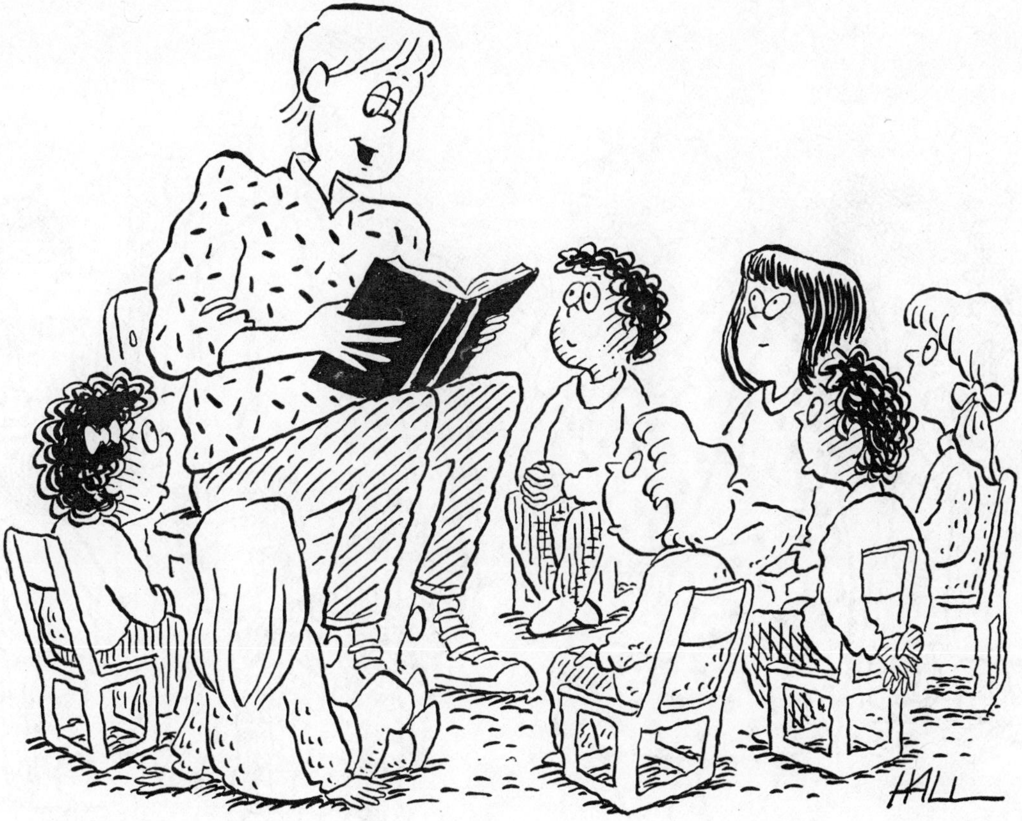
HALL

"In today's memory verse, Paul tells Timothy not to let anyone put him down because he's young... Let's make this one into a banner and hang it in the sanctuary!"

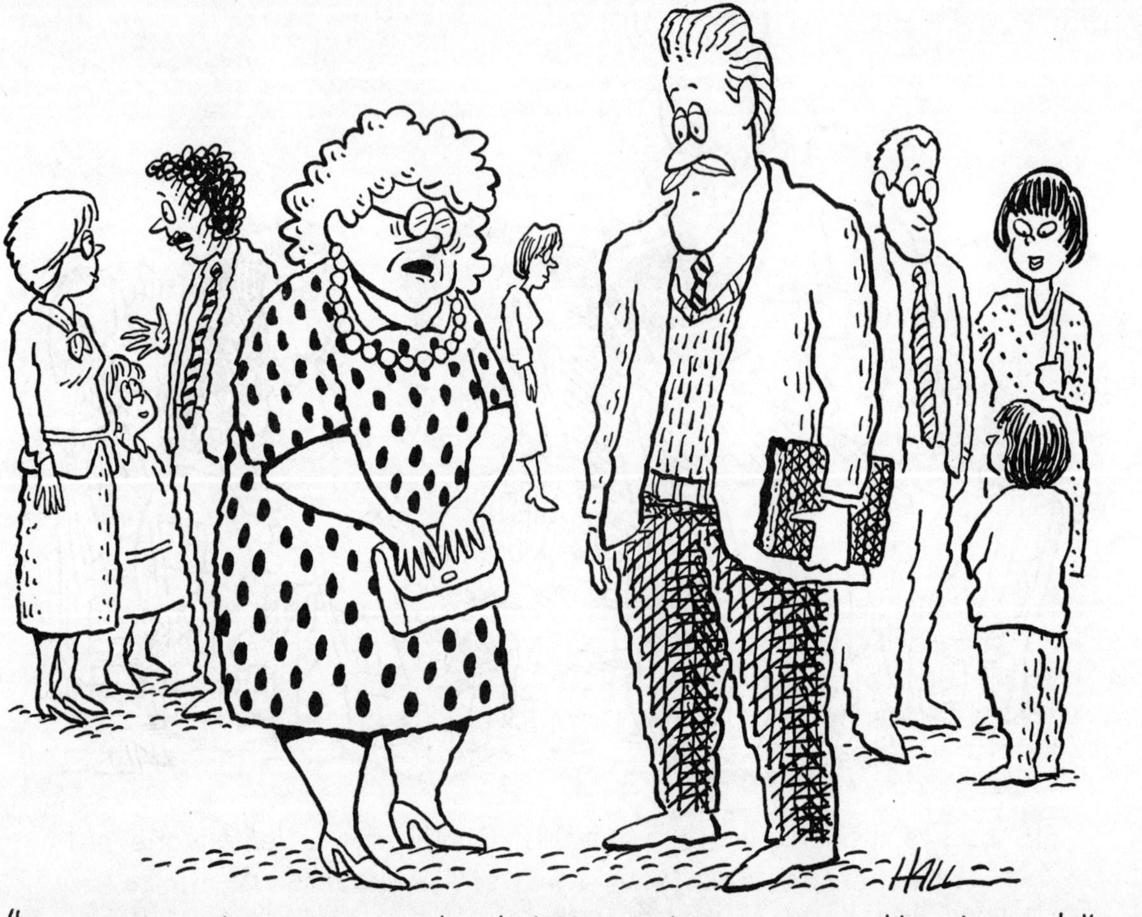
HALL
"I used to criticize the pastor, but now we have a committee to do it."

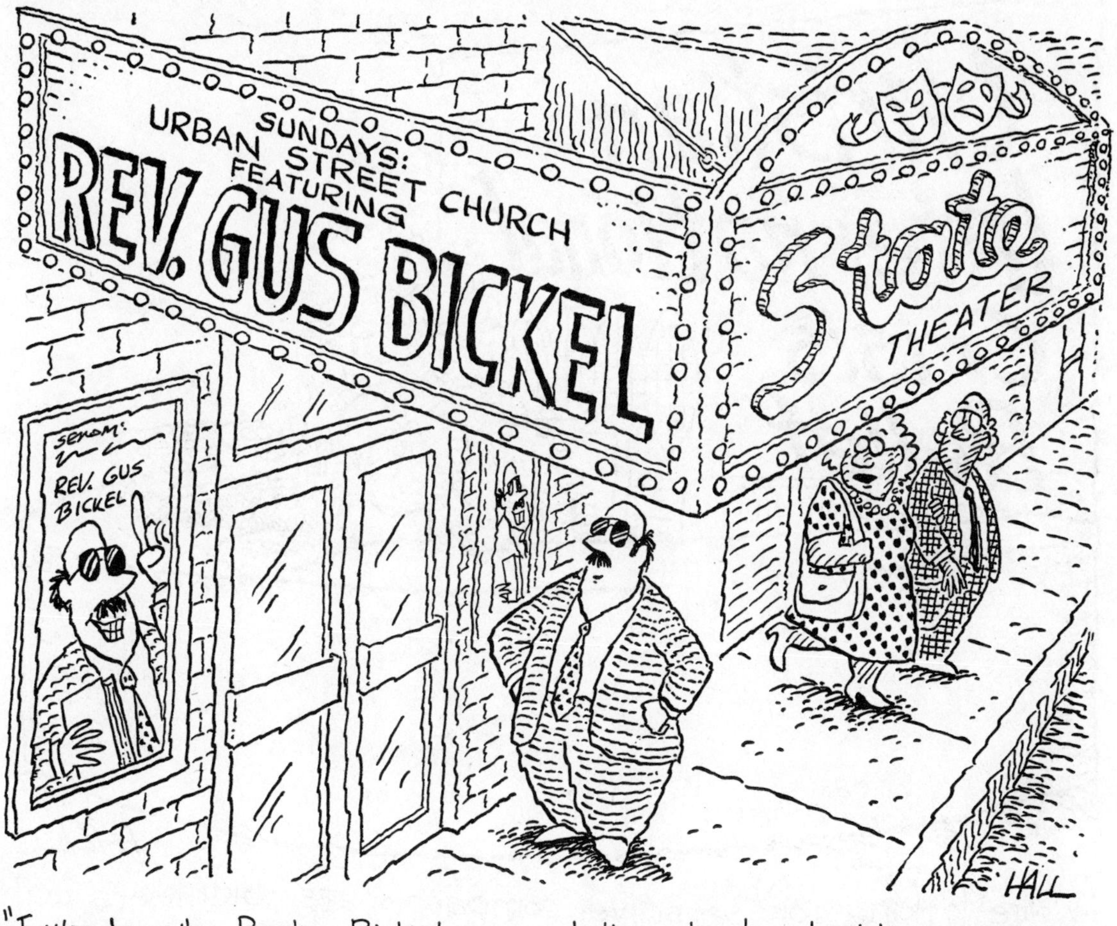
SUNDAYS:
URBAN STREET CHURCH
FEATURING
REV. GUS BICKEL
State
THEATER
SERMON:
REV. GUS
BICKEL
HALL

"I wonder why Pastor Bickel never talks about a building campaign anymore."

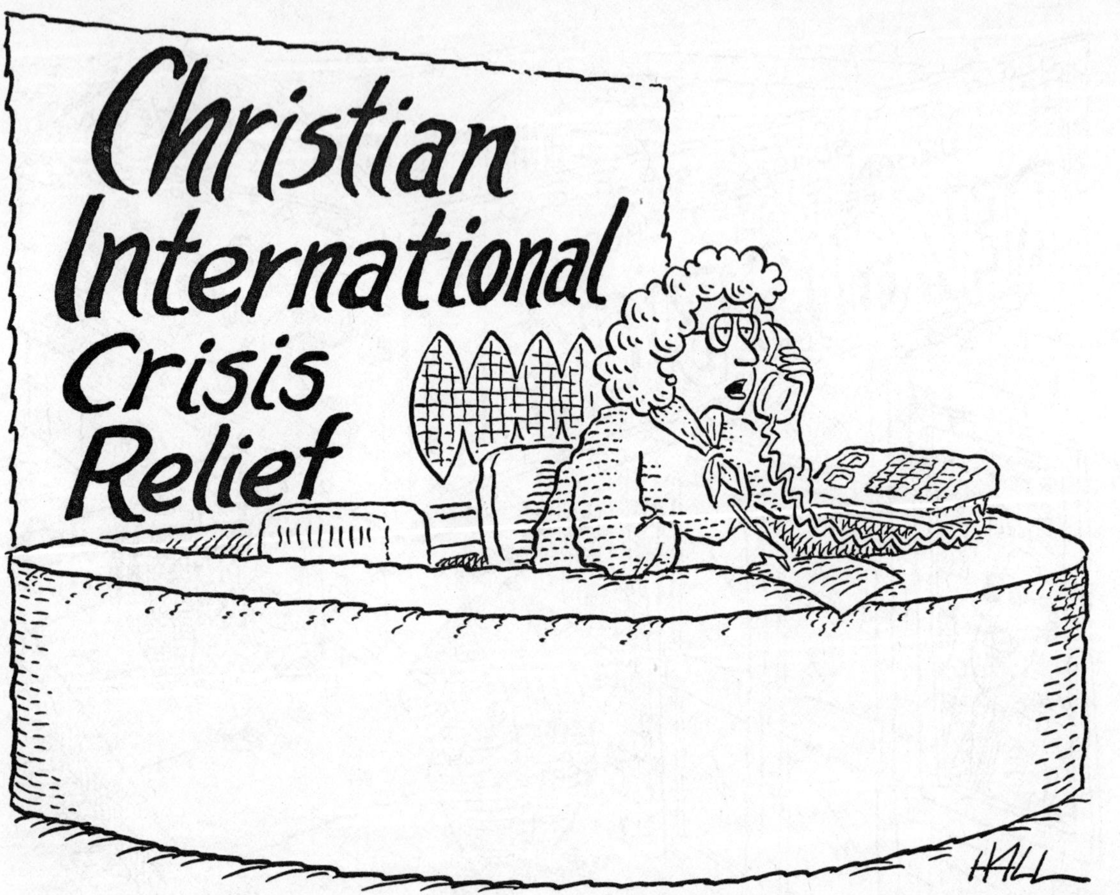
Christian
International
Crisis
Relief
HALL

"We're looking for sensitive, compassionate volunteers with experience driving armored personnel carriers."

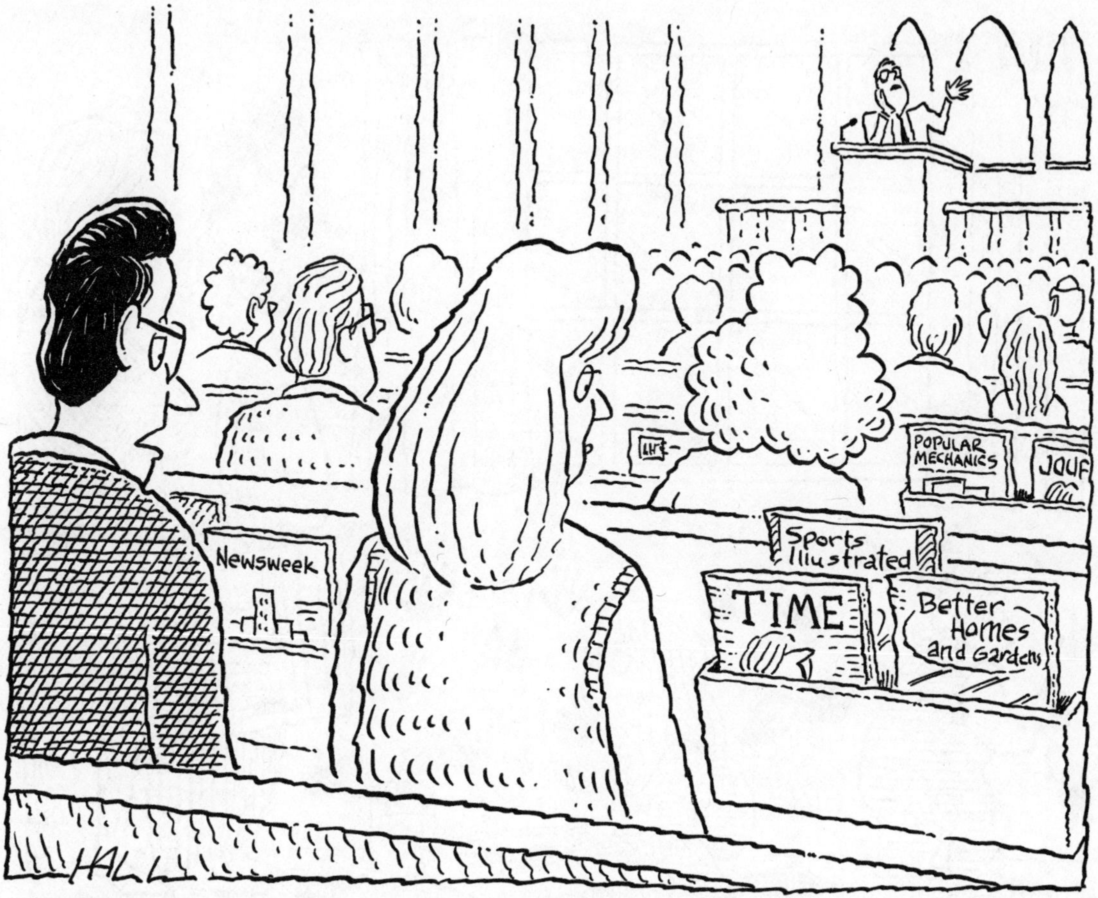
POPULAR MECHANICS
Newsweek
Sports Illustrated
TIME
Better Homes and Gardens
HALL

"I think he's given up holding our attention."

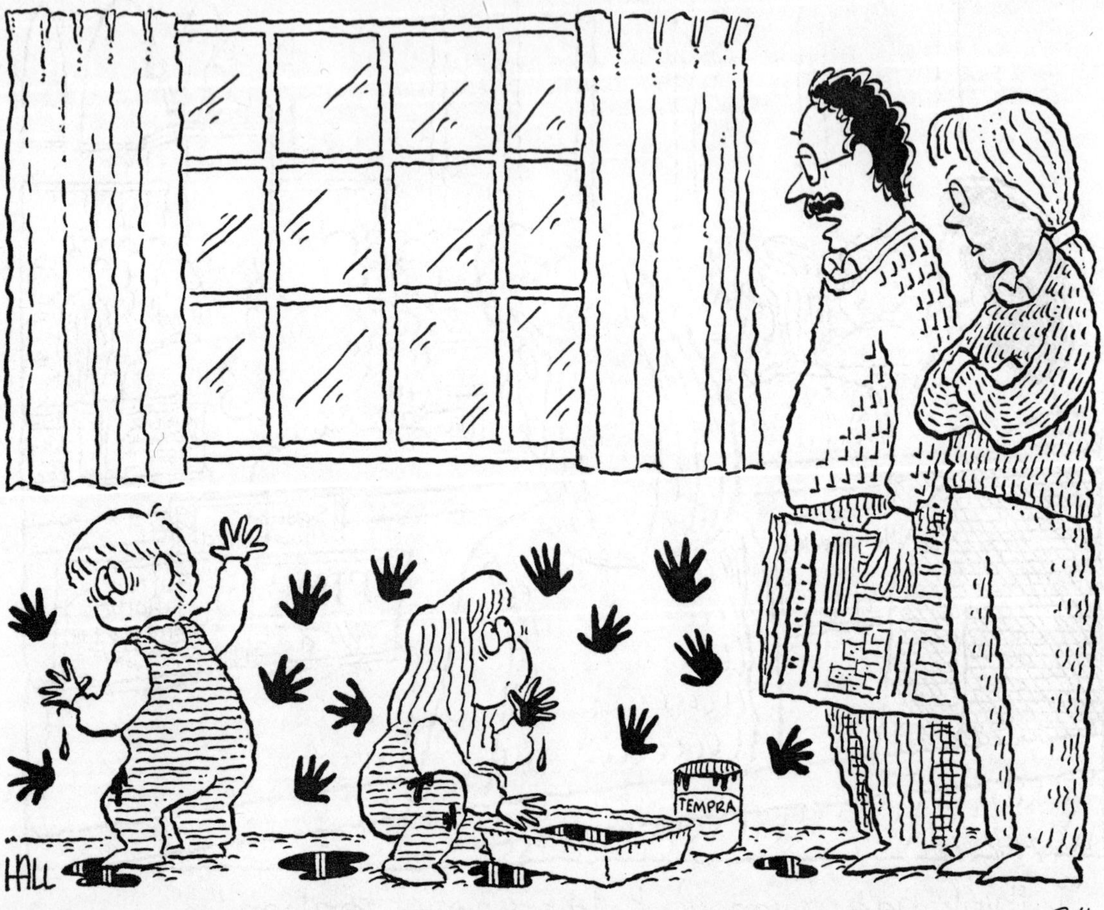
HALL
TEMPRA
"Do we discipline them or ask them to do drapes to match?"

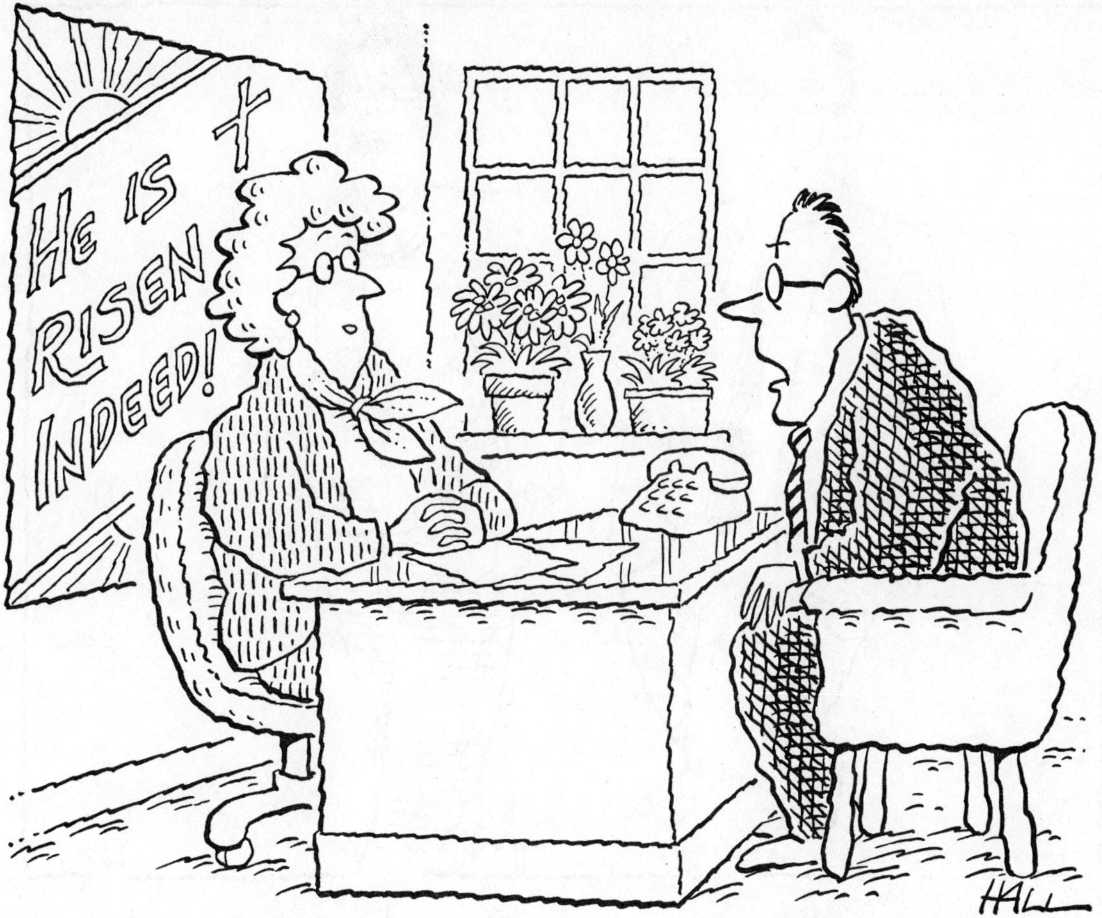
He is Risen Indeed!
HALL

"You seem to have a great love of life, Pastor. Naturally, that makes me suspicious."

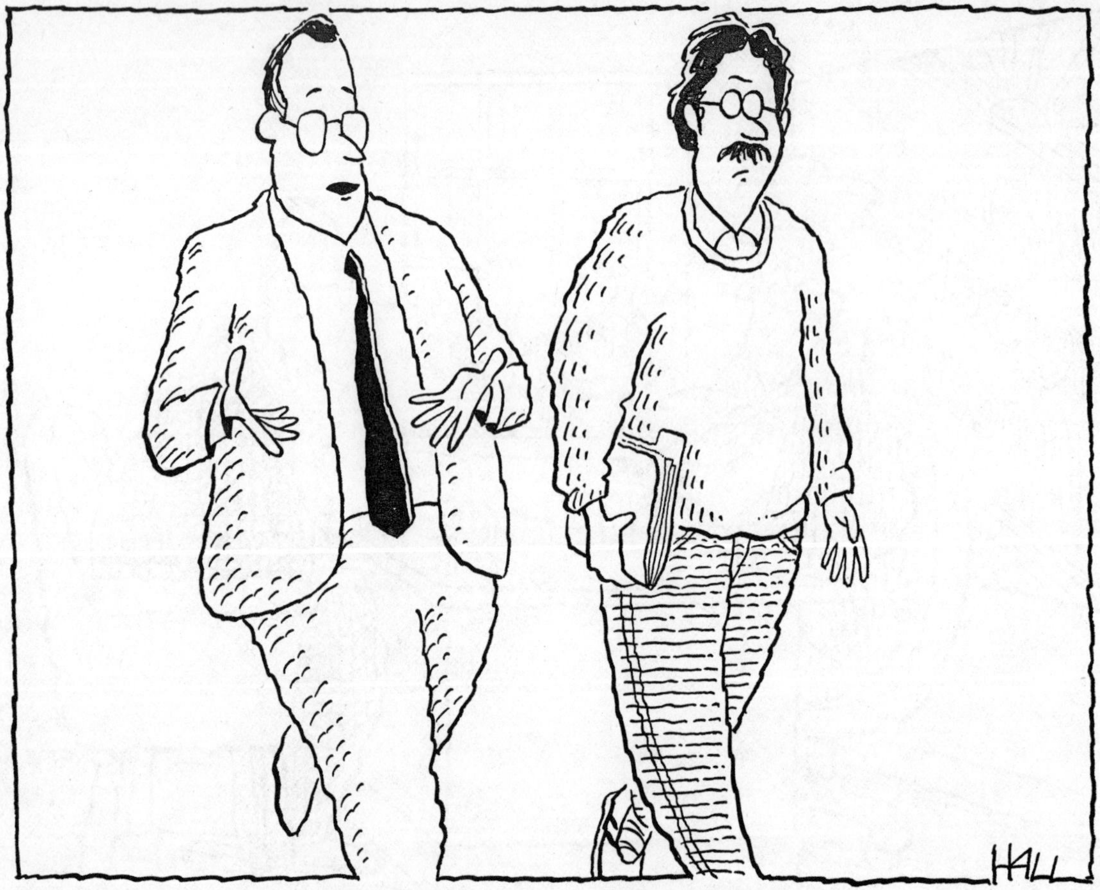
HALL

"About this year's budget.... We've decided to make youth ministry a spiritual priority instead of a financial one."

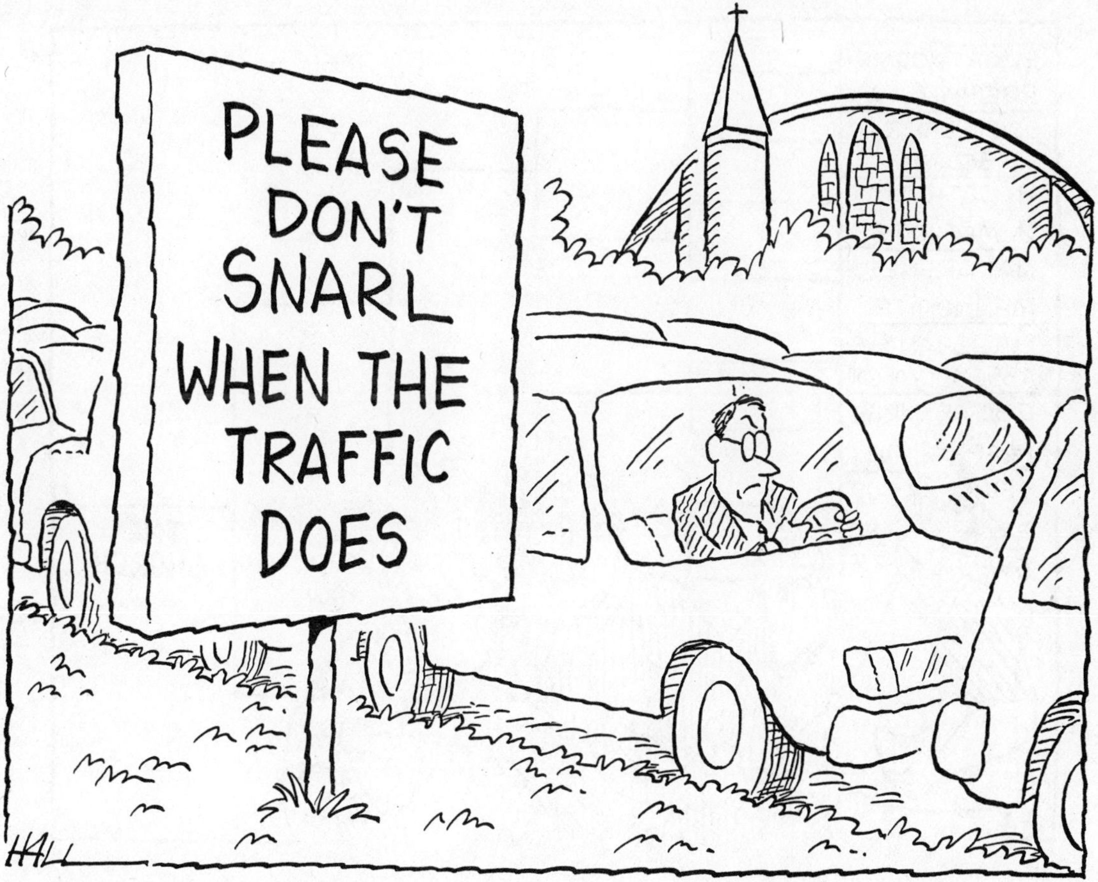
PLEASE DON'T SNARL WHEN THE TRAFFIC DOES
HALL

E. ORTHODOX
PRESBY. (USA)
SOUTHERN BAPT.
EPISCOPAL
R. CATHOLIC
U. METHODIST
NAZARENE
MENNONITE
LUTHERAN-M.S.
ASSEMBLY OF GOD
DISC. OF CHRIST
THE CHURCH
HALL

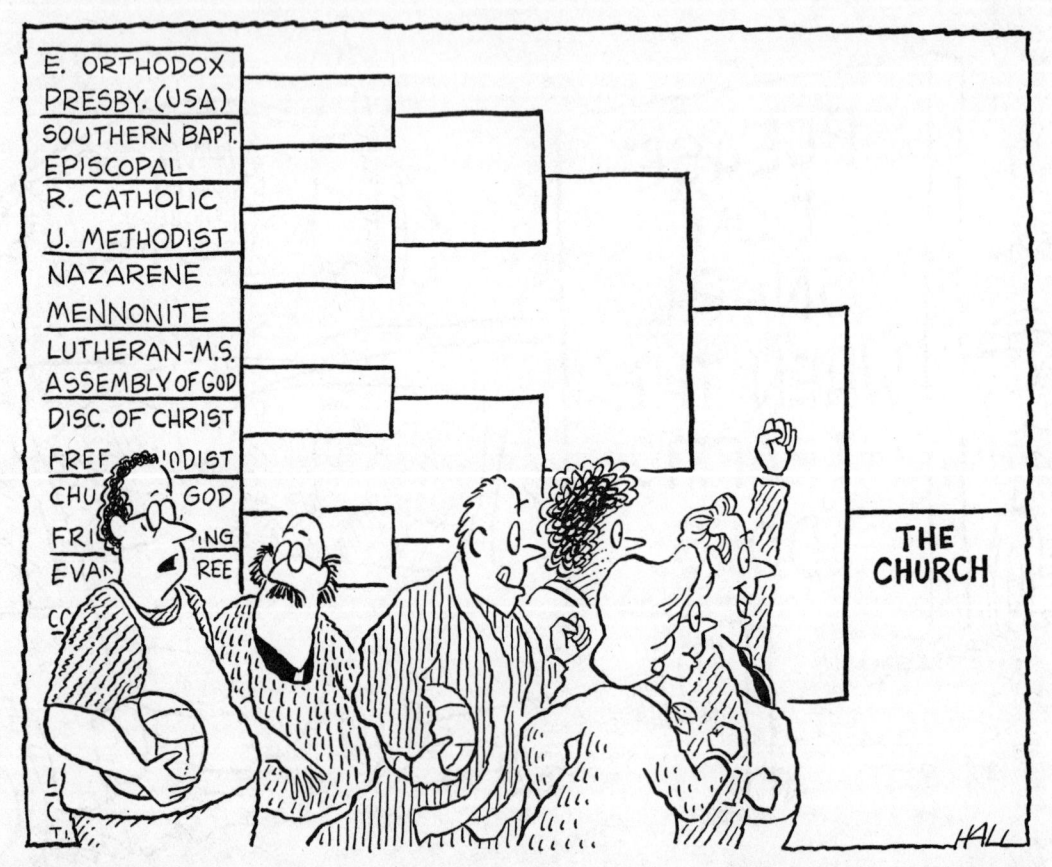

"I'd like there to be a unified Body, but is a volleyball tournament the best way to achieve it?"

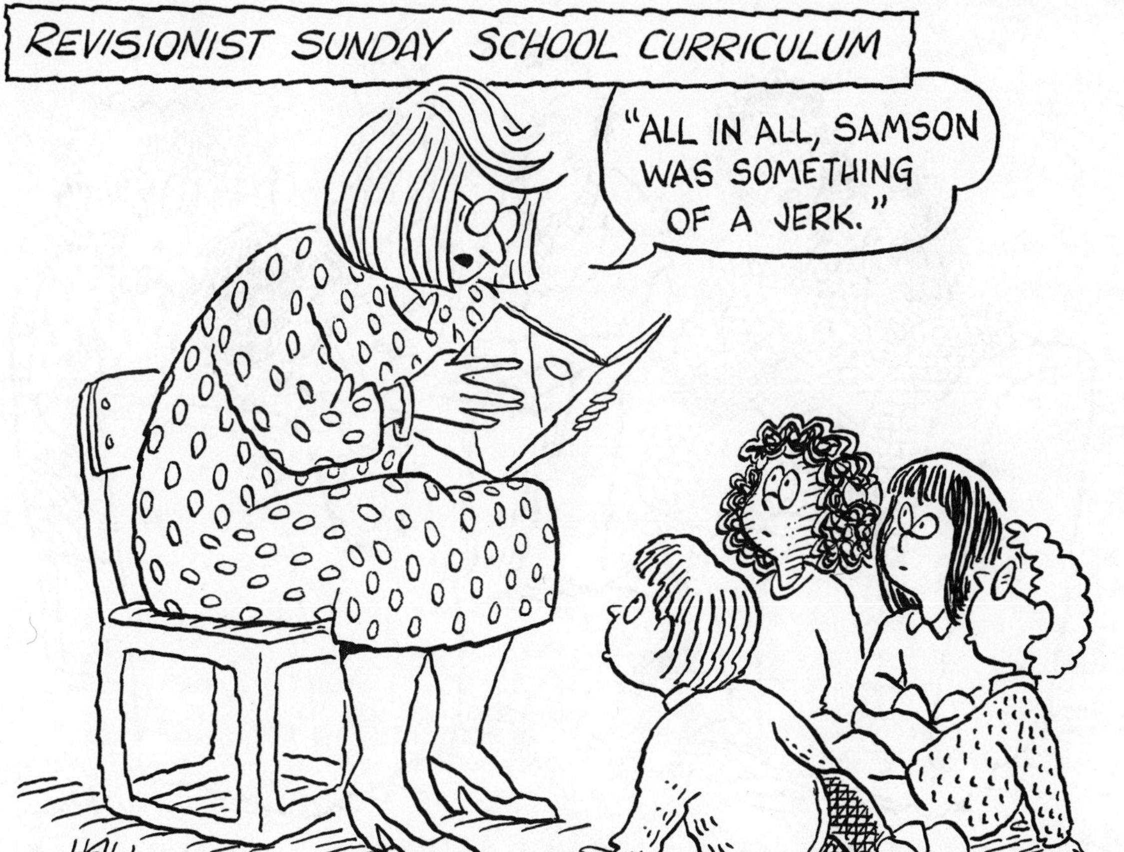
REVISIONIST SUNDAY SCHOOL CURRICULUM
"ALL IN ALL, SAMSON WAS SOMETHING OF A JERK."
HALL

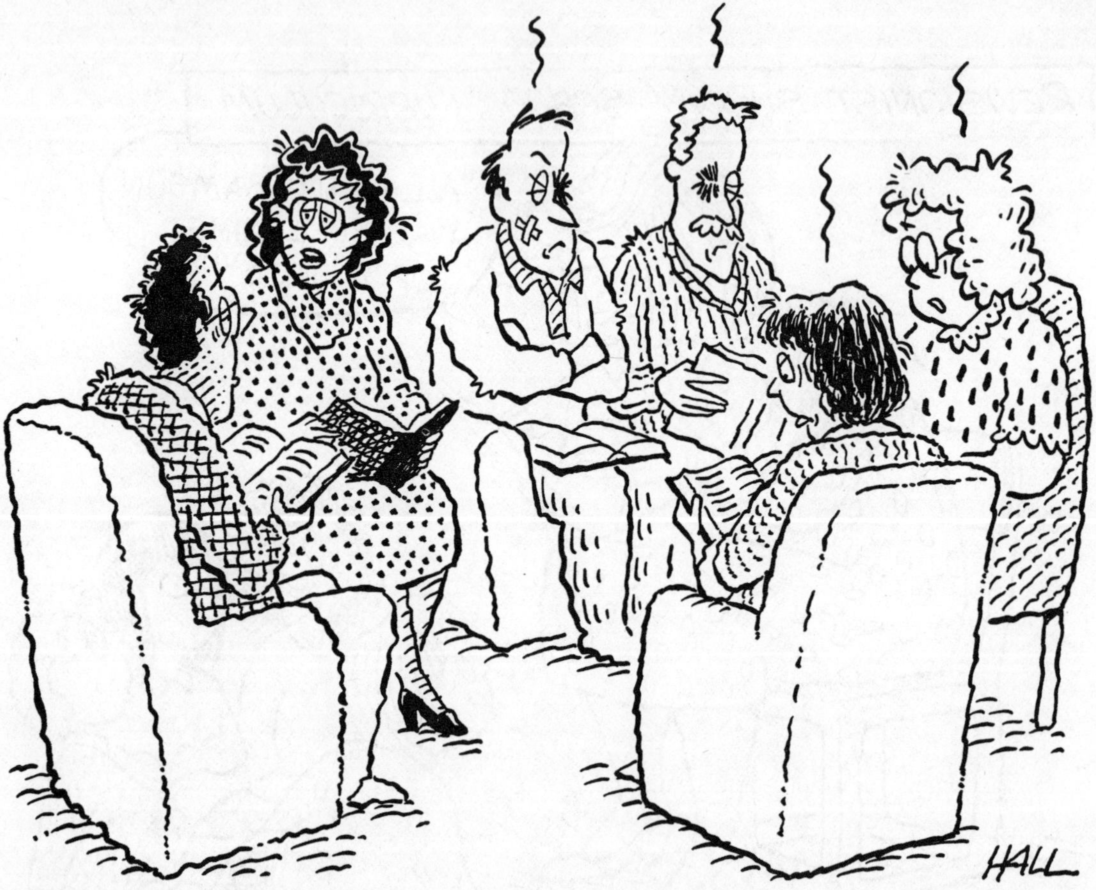
HALL

"Next time, let's make sure the ice-breaker doesn't include questions about politics."

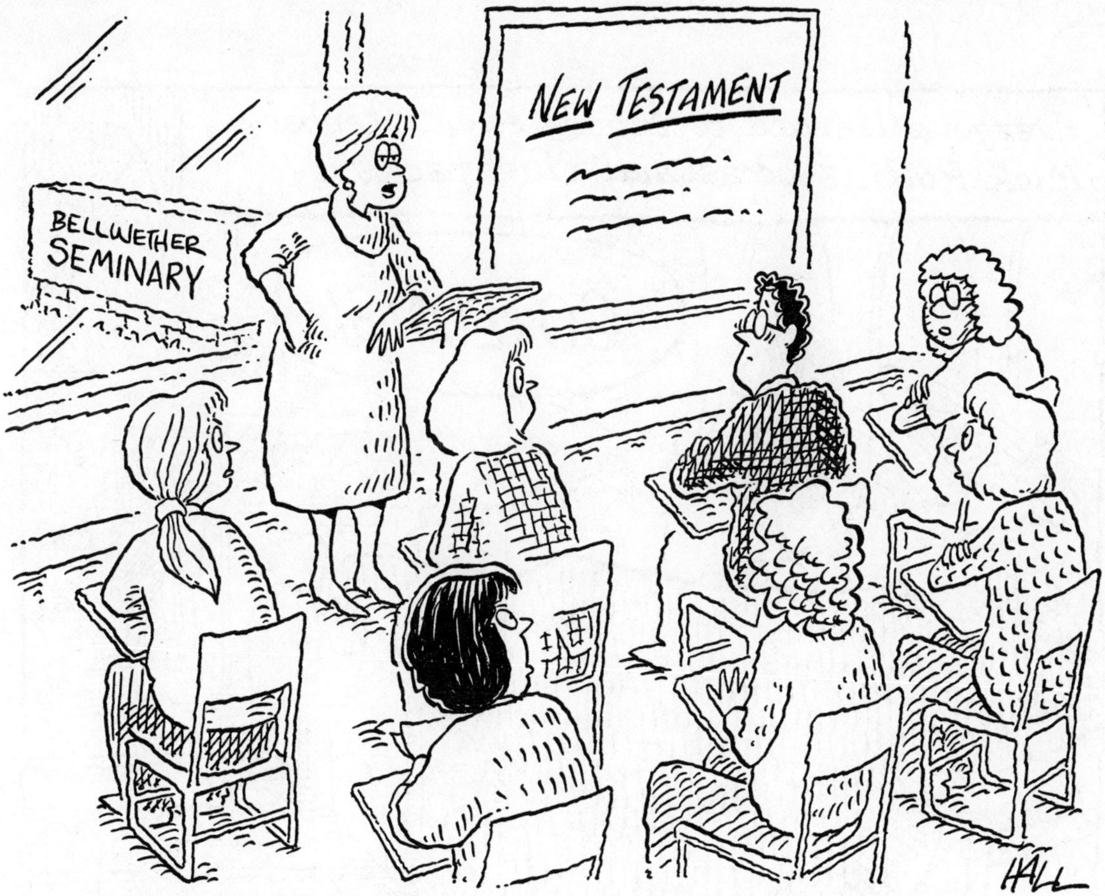
NEW TESTAMENT
BELLWETHER SEMINARY
HALL
"Does anyone besides Larry want to debate the role of women in ministry?"

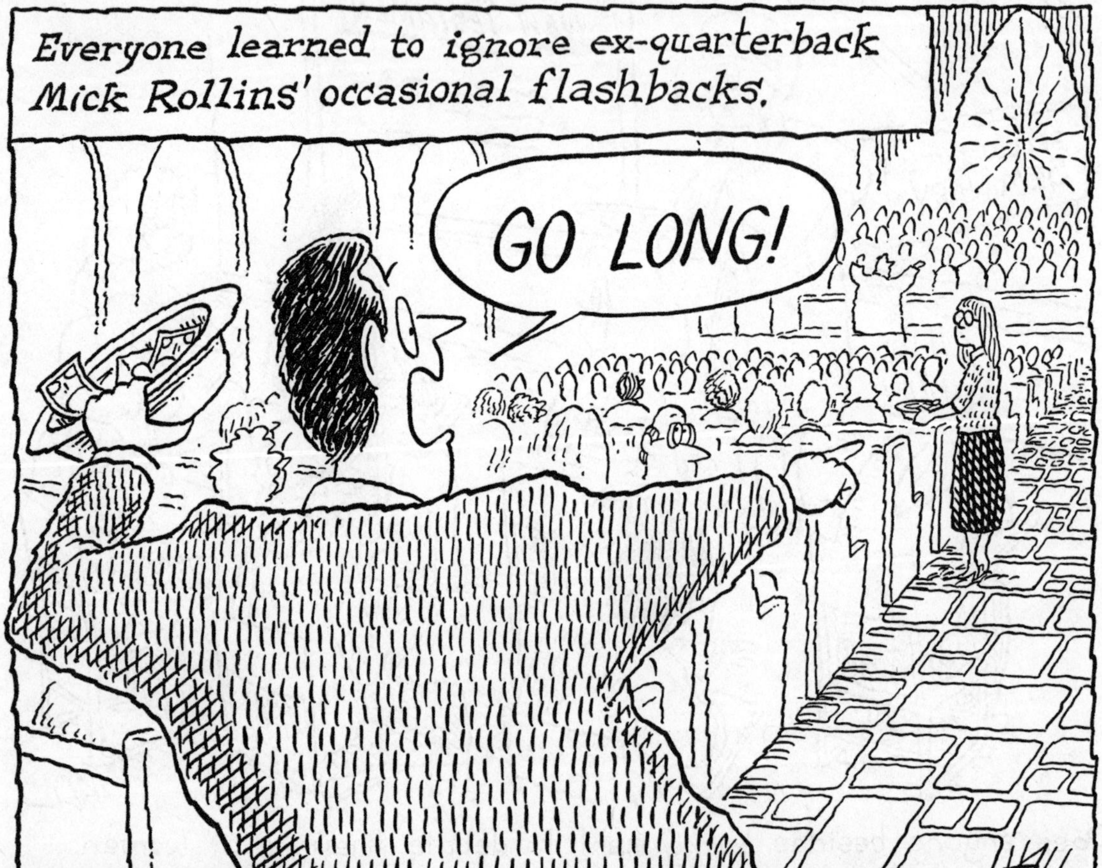
Everyone learned to ignore ex-quarterback Mick Rollins' occasional flashbacks.
GO LONG!
HALL

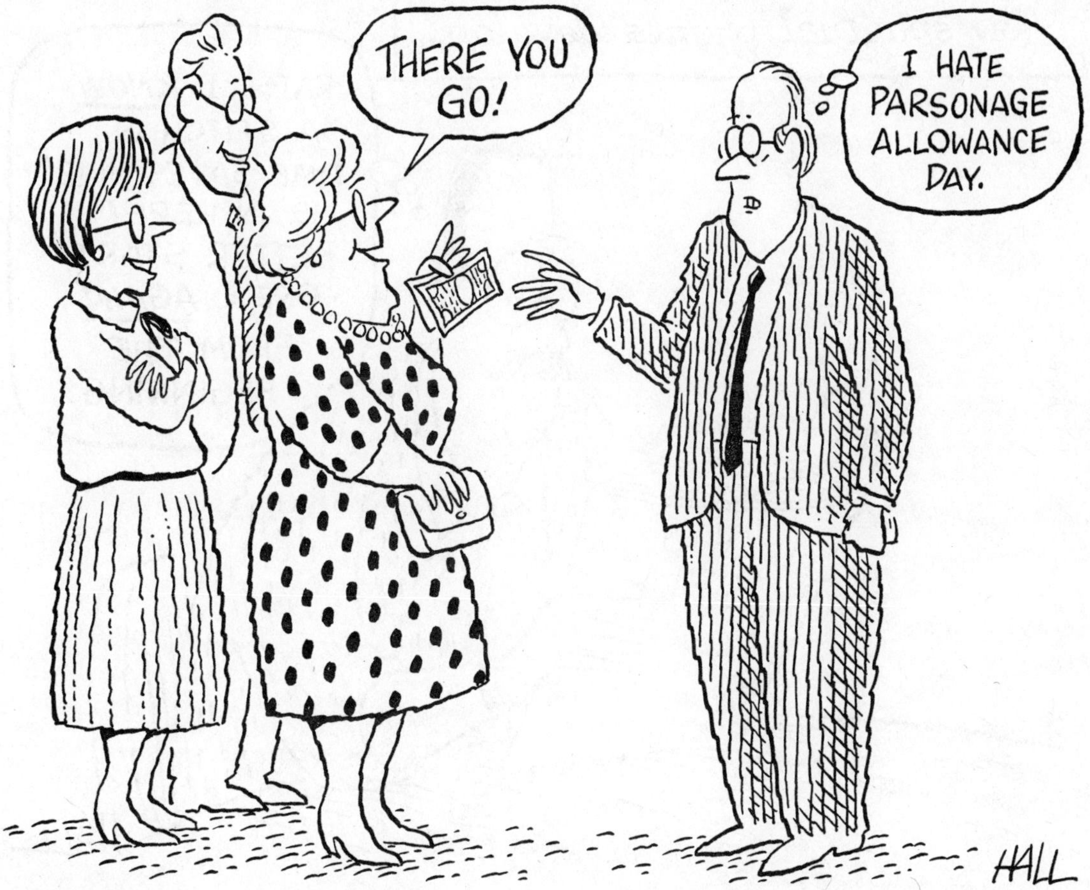
THERE YOU GO!
I HATE PARSONAGE ALLOWANCE DAY.
HALL

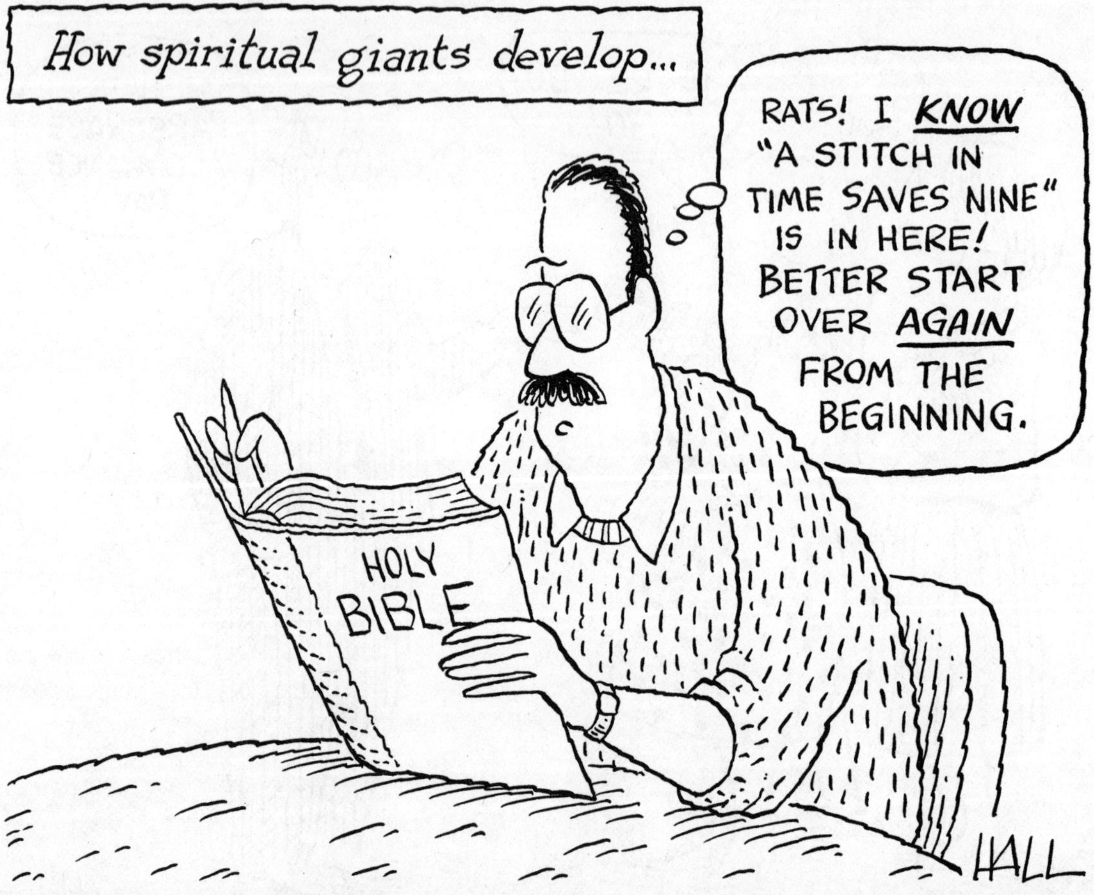
How spiritual giants develop...
RATS! I KNOW "A STITCH IN TIME SAVES NINE" IS IN HERE! BETTER START OVER AGAIN FROM THE BEGINNING.
HOLY BIBLE
HALL

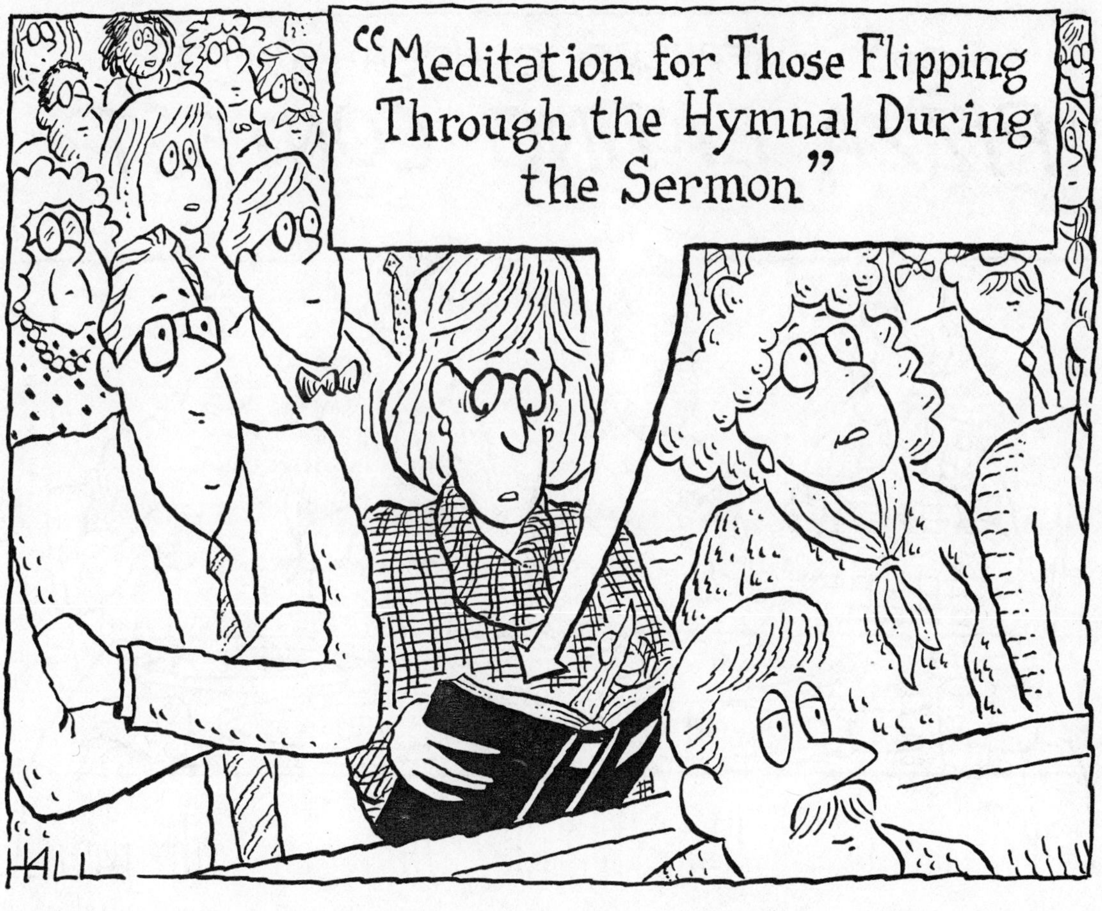
"Meditation for Those Flipping Through the Hymnal During the Sermon"
HALL

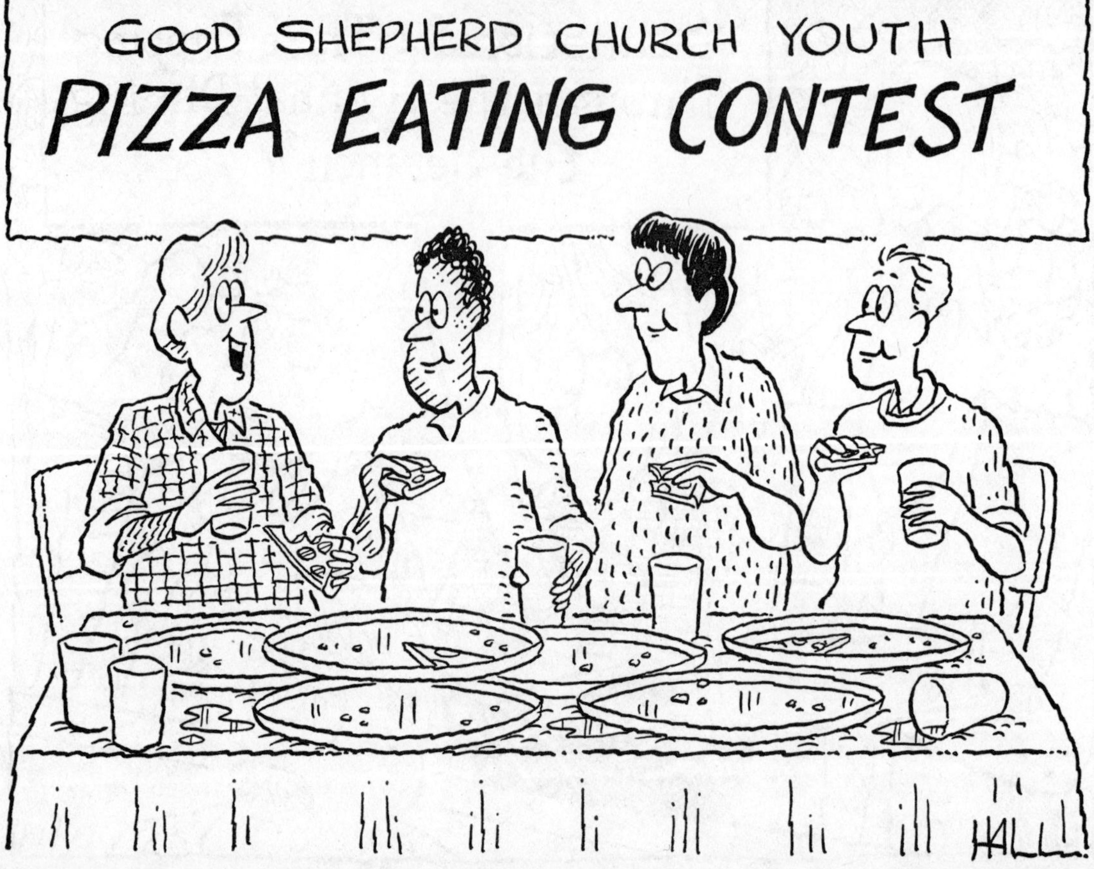
GOOD SHEPHERD CHURCH YOUTH
PIZZA EATING CONTEST
HALL

"Maybe we could get some other churches to start a league!"

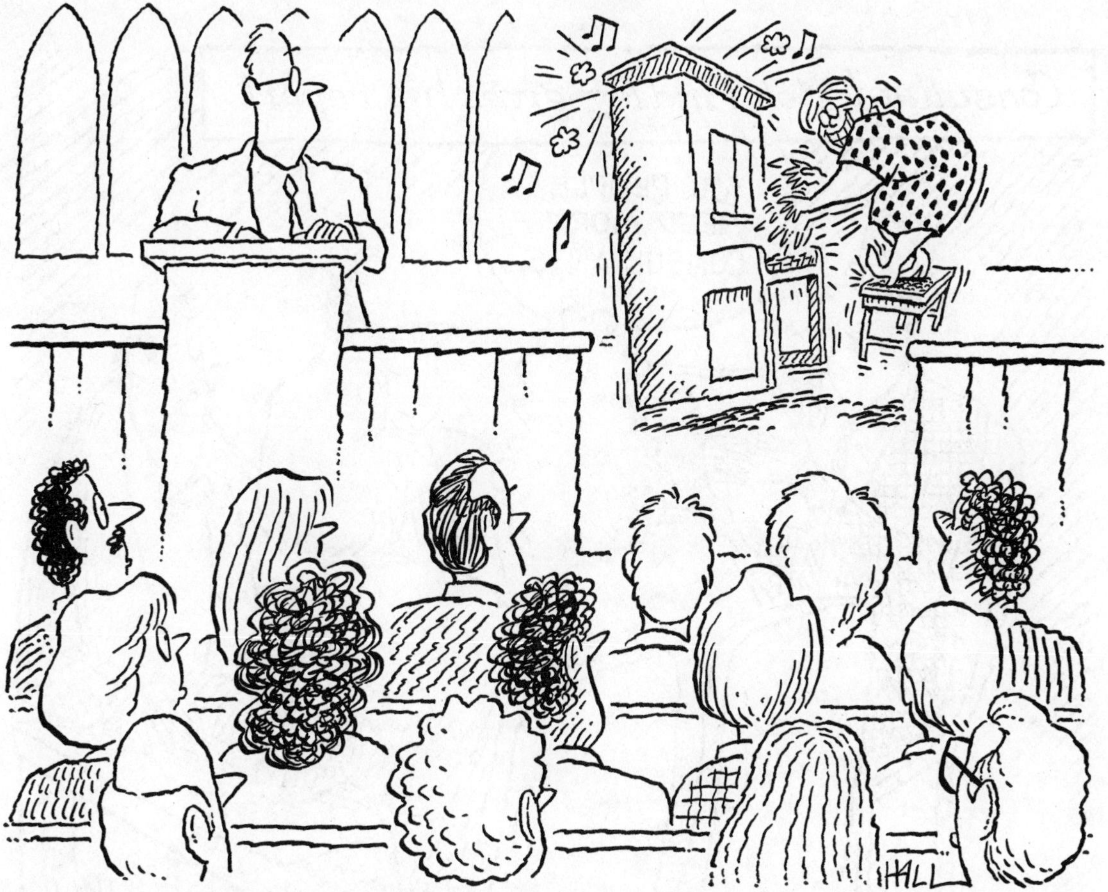
HALL

People began to suspect that Emily had been attending too many music workshops.

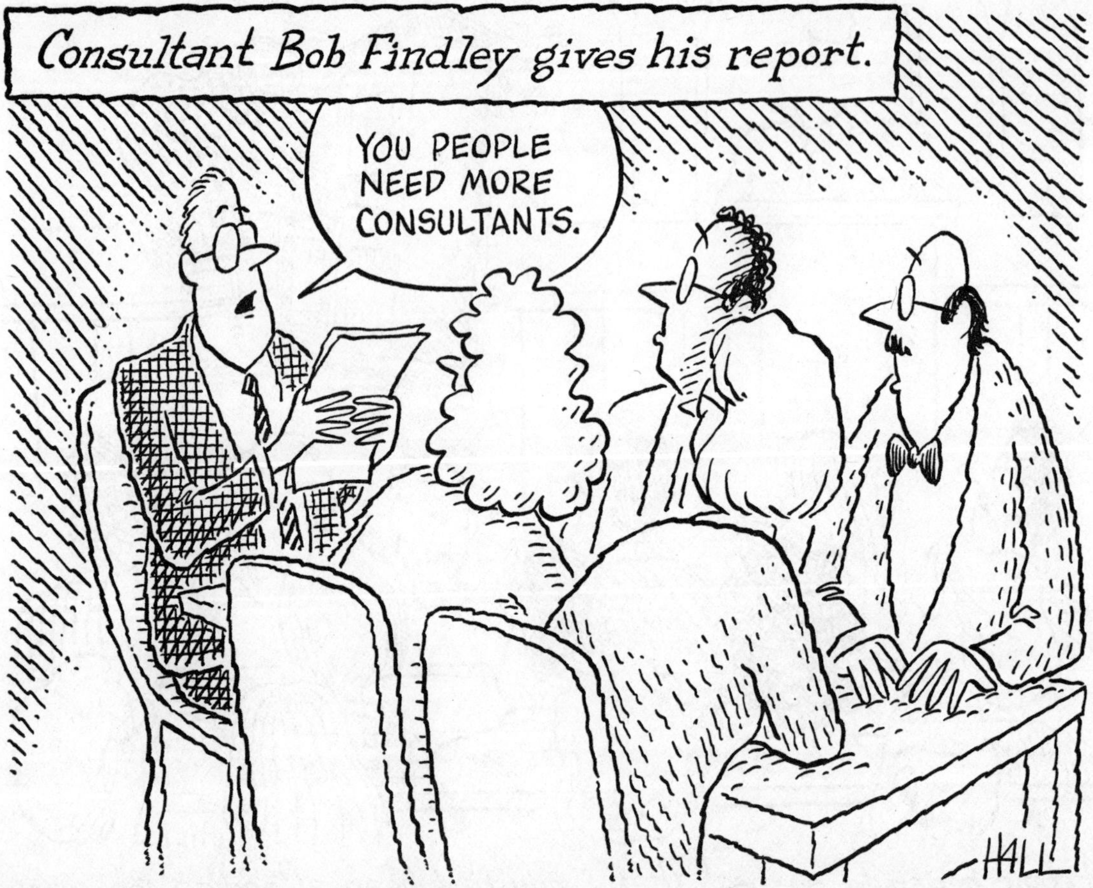
Consultant Bob Findley gives his report.
YOU PEOPLE NEED MORE CONSULTANTS.
HALL

"You weren't exactly breaking the law, but I assume you want to be held to a higher standard."

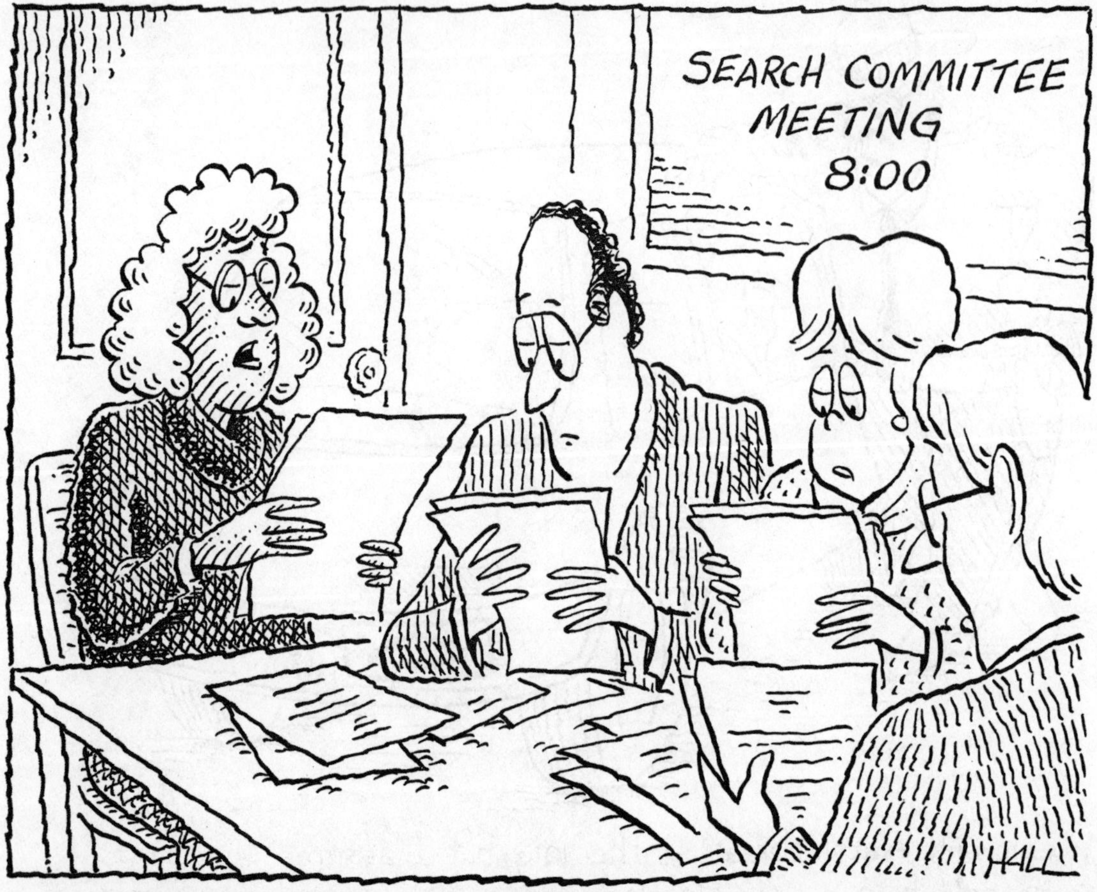
SEARCH COMMITTEE
MEETING
8:00
HALL

"I feel uneasy when a candidate brags about being unindicted."

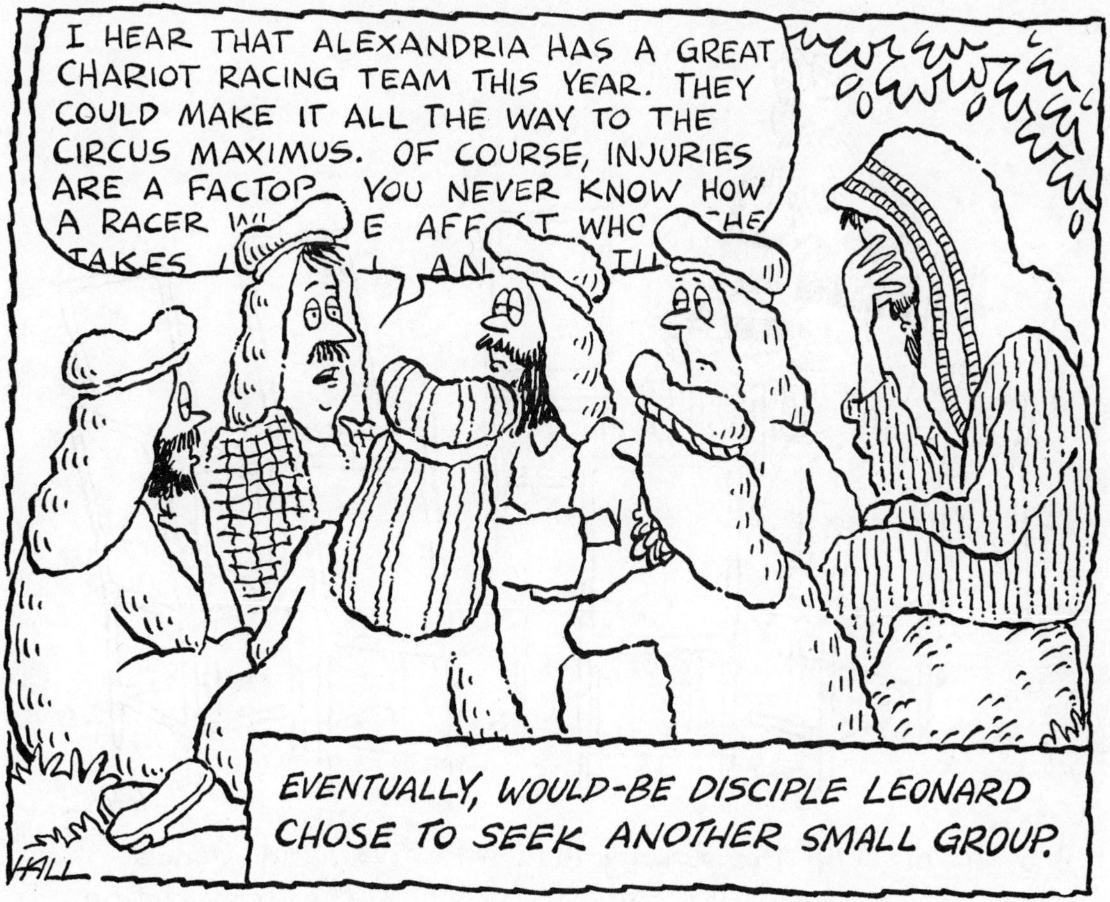
I HEAR THAT ALEXANDRIA HAS A GREAT CHARIOT RACING TEAM THIS YEAR. THEY COULD MAKE IT ALL THE WAY TO THE CIRCUS MAXIMUS. OF COURSE, INJURIES ARE A FACTOR. YOU NEVER KNOW HOW A RACER
EVENTUALLY, WOULD-BE DISCIPLE LEONARD CHOSE TO SEEK ANOTHER SMALL GROUP.
HALL

It's the night of the County Mildew Festival, and Gene's study of 2 Chronicles fails to weather the competition.

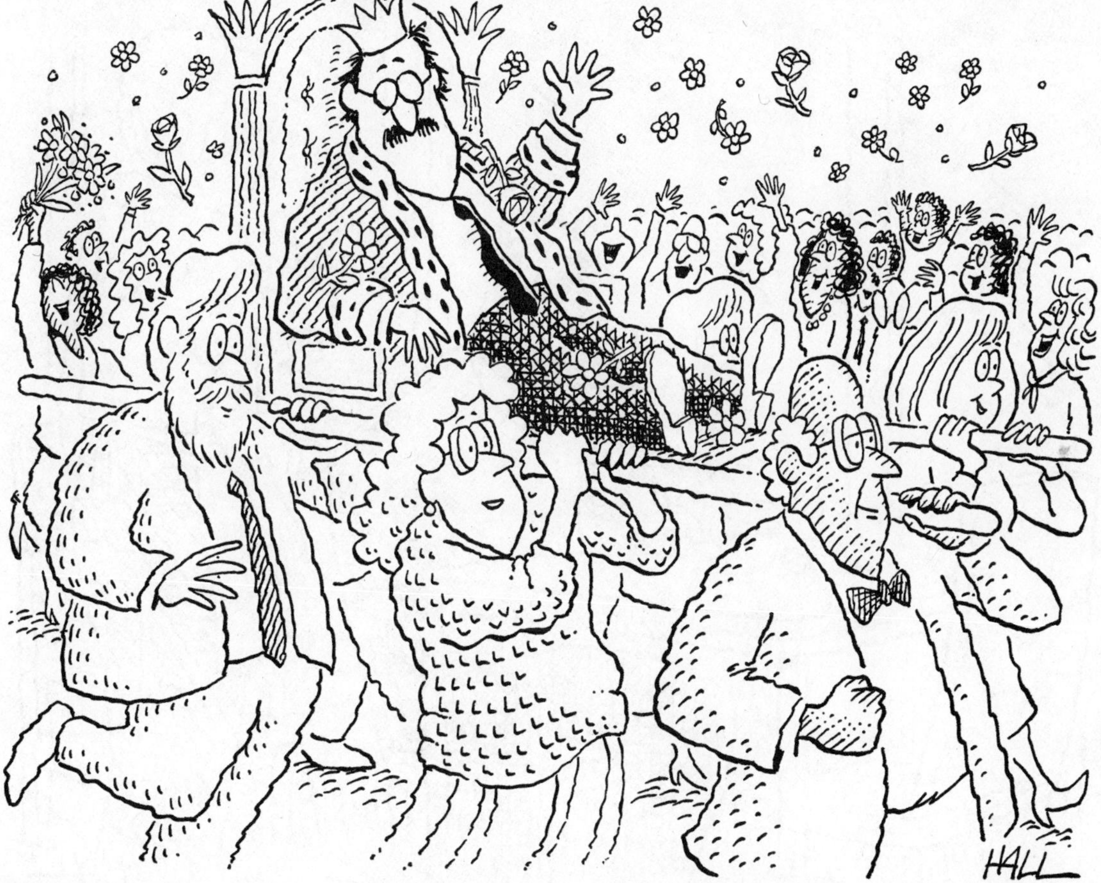
HALL
Transition tip: When assuming a new pastorate, put up with local rituals.

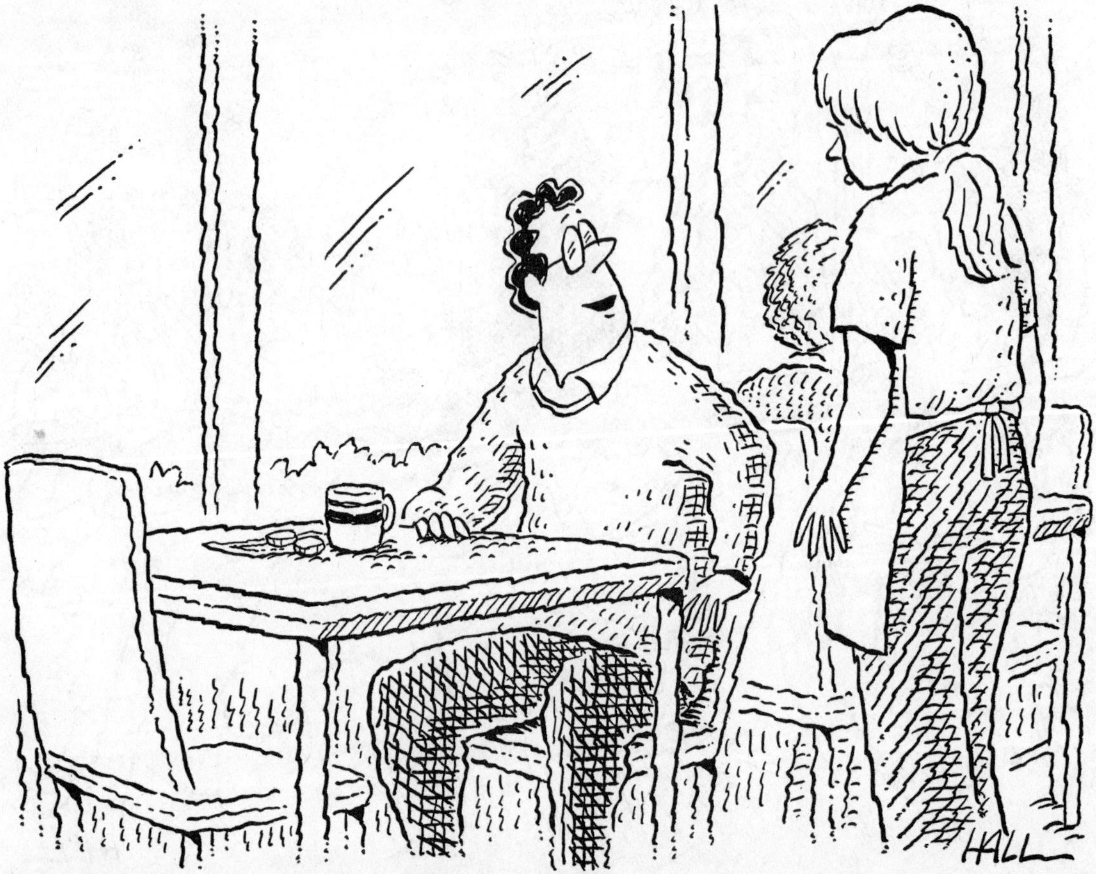
HALL

"I left a 20% tip. Please consider it lifestyle evangelism."

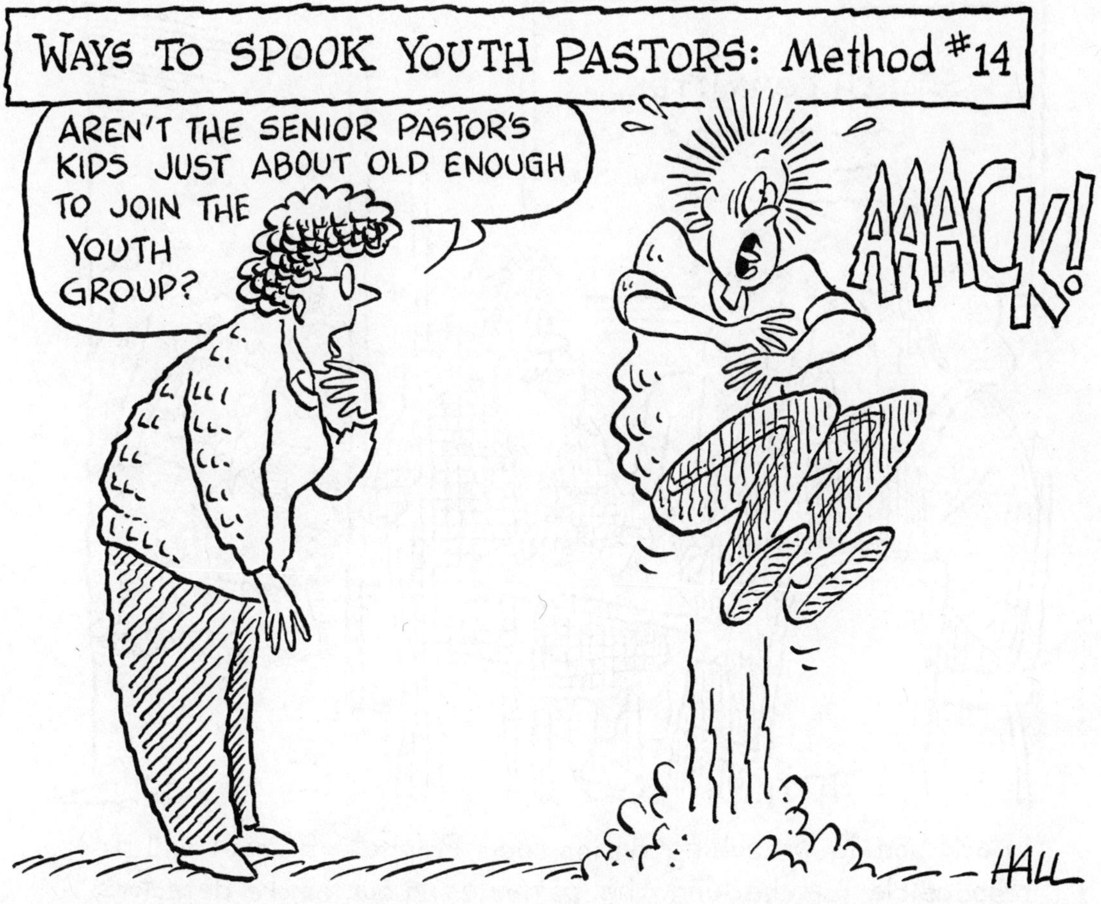

WAYS TO SPOOK YOUTH PASTORS: Method #14
AREN'T THE SENIOR PASTOR'S KIDS JUST ABOUT OLD ENOUGH TO JOIN THE YOUTH GROUP?
AAACK!
HALL

"In addition to preaching duties, our Prophet of Doom will be responsible for checking the batteries in our smoke detectors."

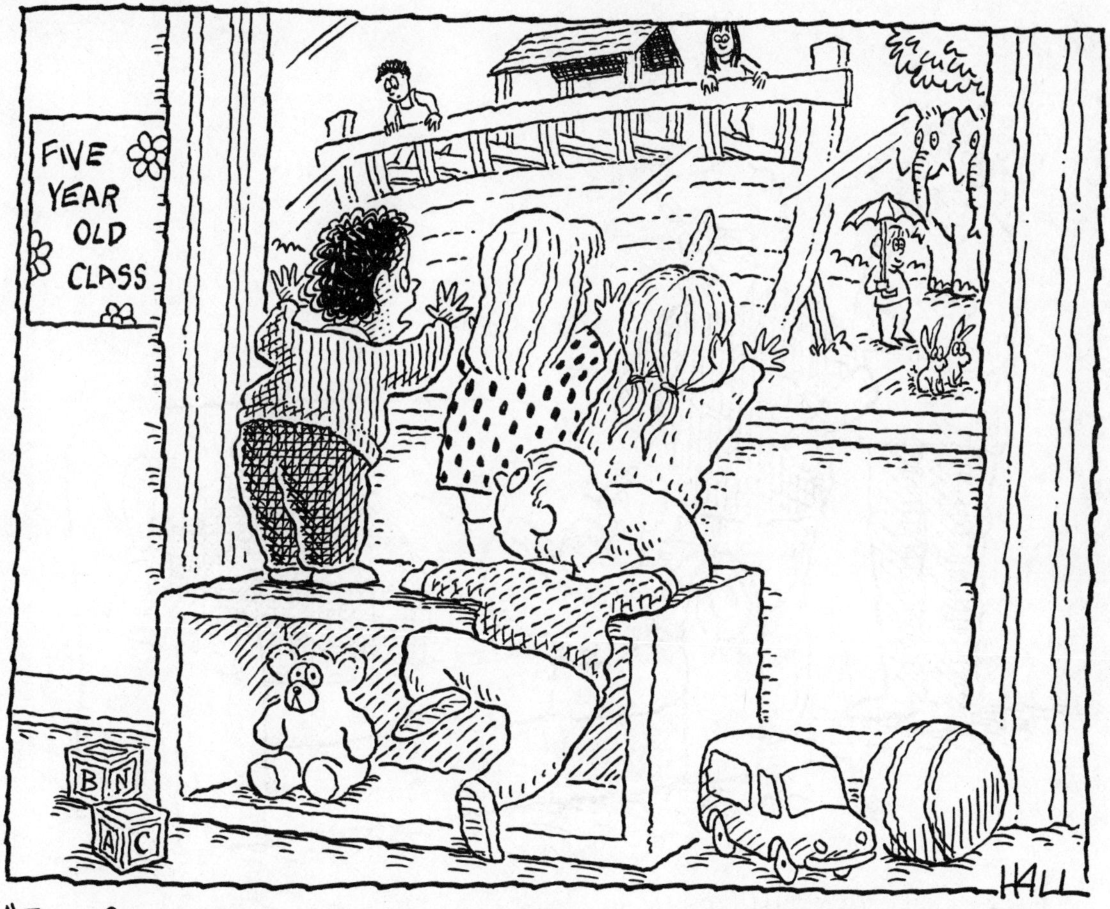
FIVE YEAR OLD CLASS
B N
A C
HALL

"The first graders always seem to know something we don't."

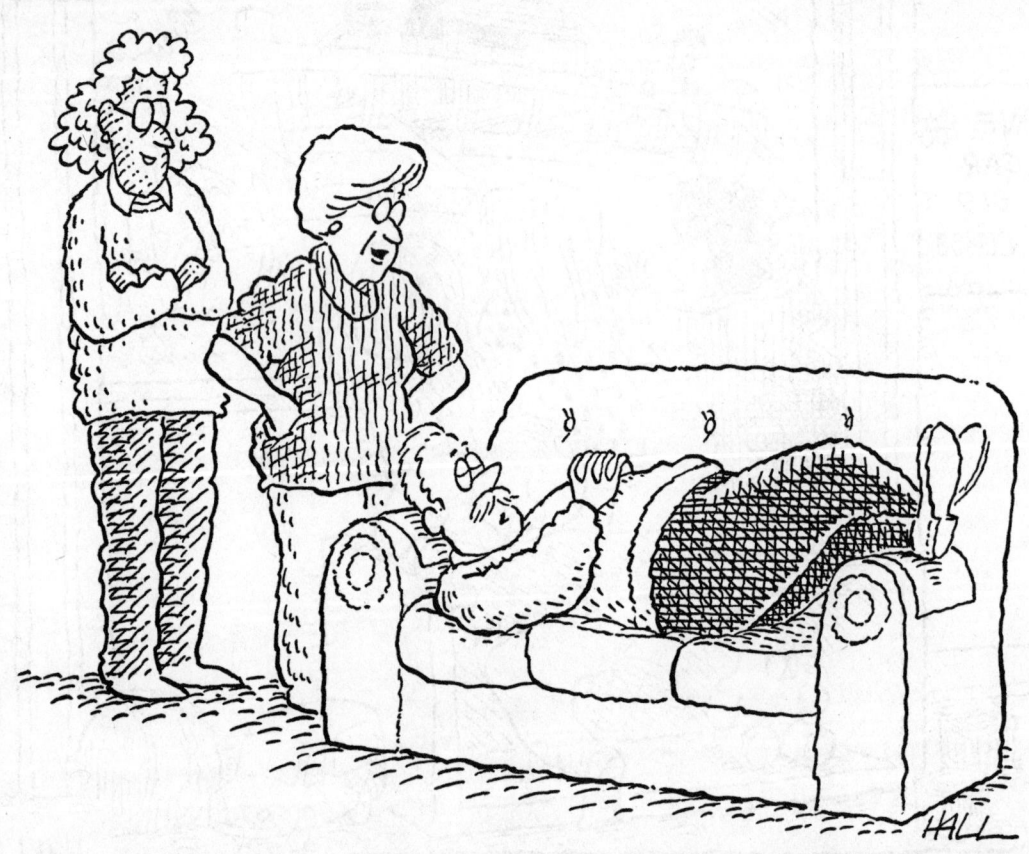

"I may not have the faith to move mountains, but sometimes I can get Stan off the couch."

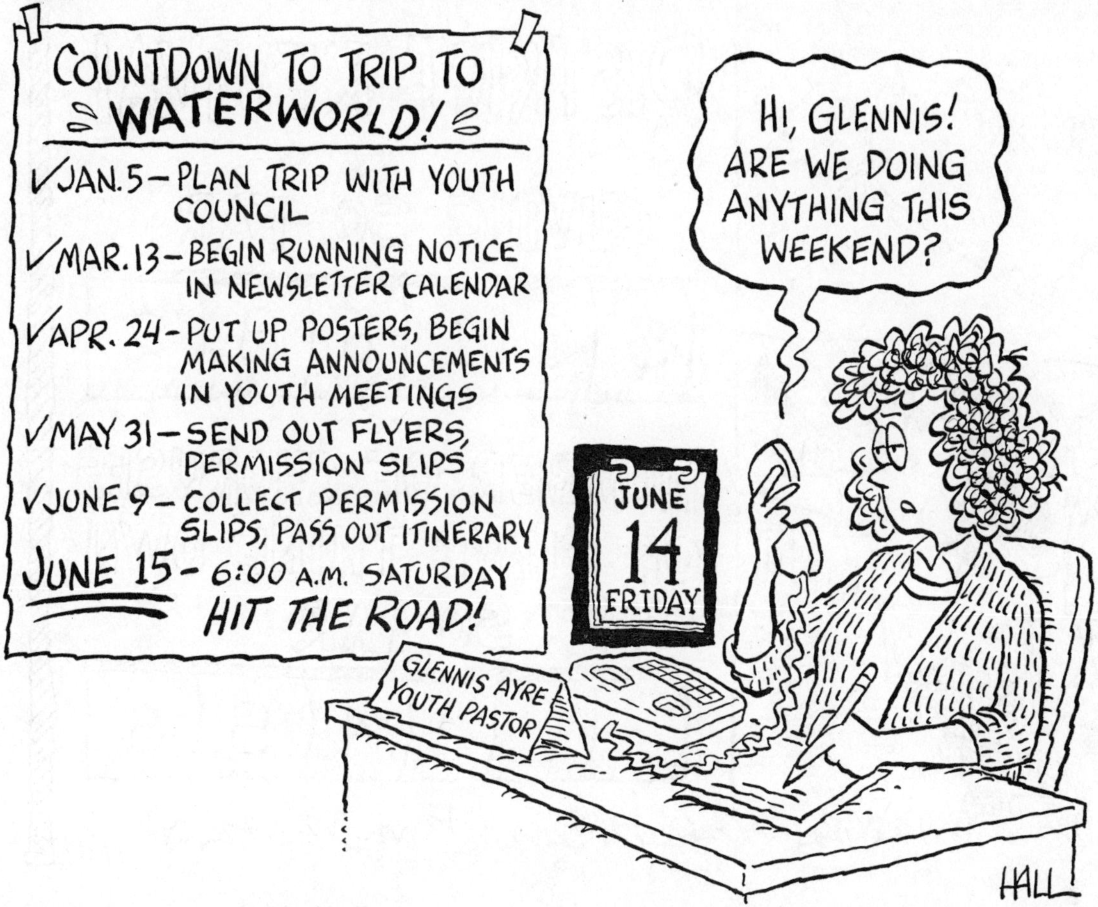
COUNTDOWN TO TRIP TO WATERWORLD!
✓JAN. 5 – PLAN TRIP WITH YOUTH COUNCIL
✓MAR. 13 – BEGIN RUNNING NOTICE IN NEWSLETTER CALENDAR
✓APR. 24 – PUT UP POSTERS, BEGIN MAKING ANNOUNCEMENTS IN YOUTH MEETINGS
✓MAY 31 – SEND OUT FLYERS, PERMISSION SLIPS
✓JUNE 9 – COLLECT PERMISSION SLIPS, PASS OUT ITINERARY
JUNE 15 – 6:00 A.M. SATURDAY HIT THE ROAD!
JUNE 14 FRIDAY
GLENNIS AYRE YOUTH PASTOR
HI, GLENNIS! ARE WE DOING ANYTHING THIS WEEKEND?
HALL

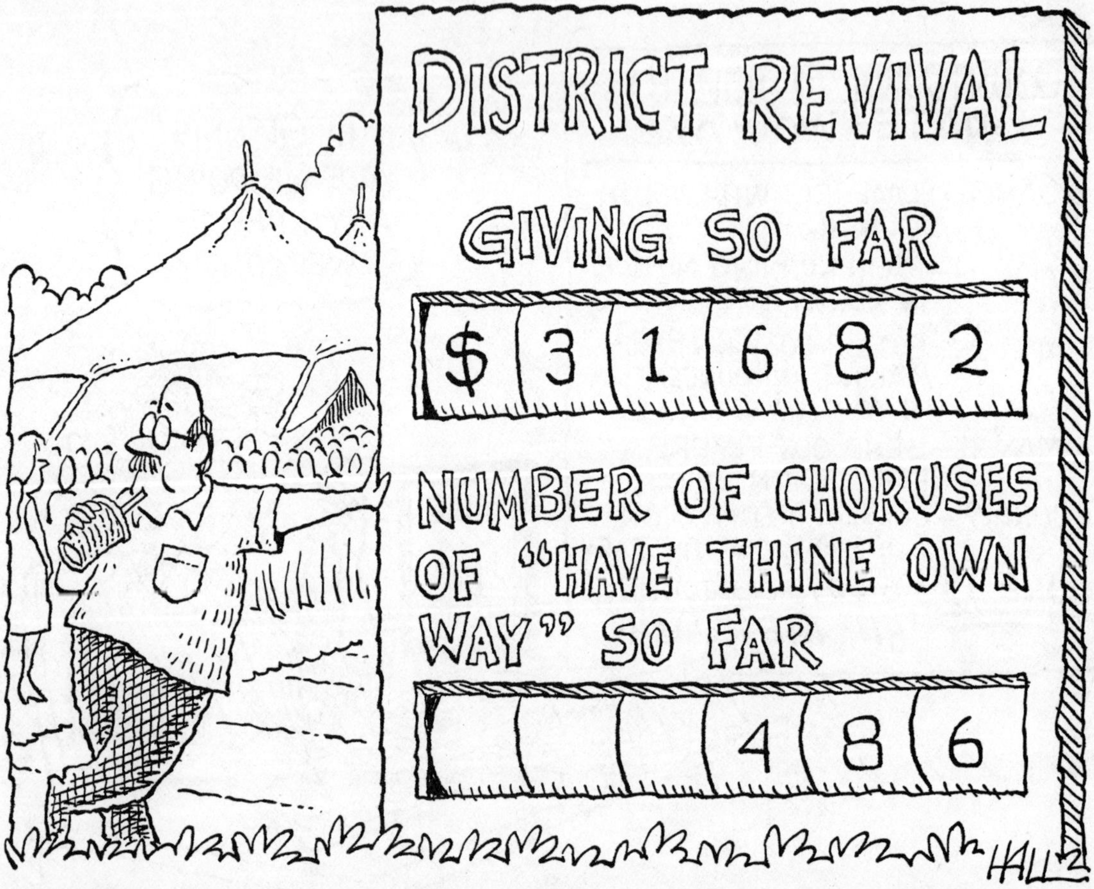
DISTRICT REVIVAL
GIVING SO FAR
$ 3 1 6 8 2
NUMBER OF CHORUSES OF "HAVE THINE OWN WAY" SO FAR
4 8 6
HALL

Feeling guilty about his role in the commercialization of Christmas, Santa Claus switches from toys to tracts.

"Everyone is really with her today."

"Did Jim *really* leave the group because of a scheduling conflict, or was it because we couldn't accept a non-rodent?"

TODAY'S EVENT: FEEDING CHRISTIANS TO LIONS
HALL

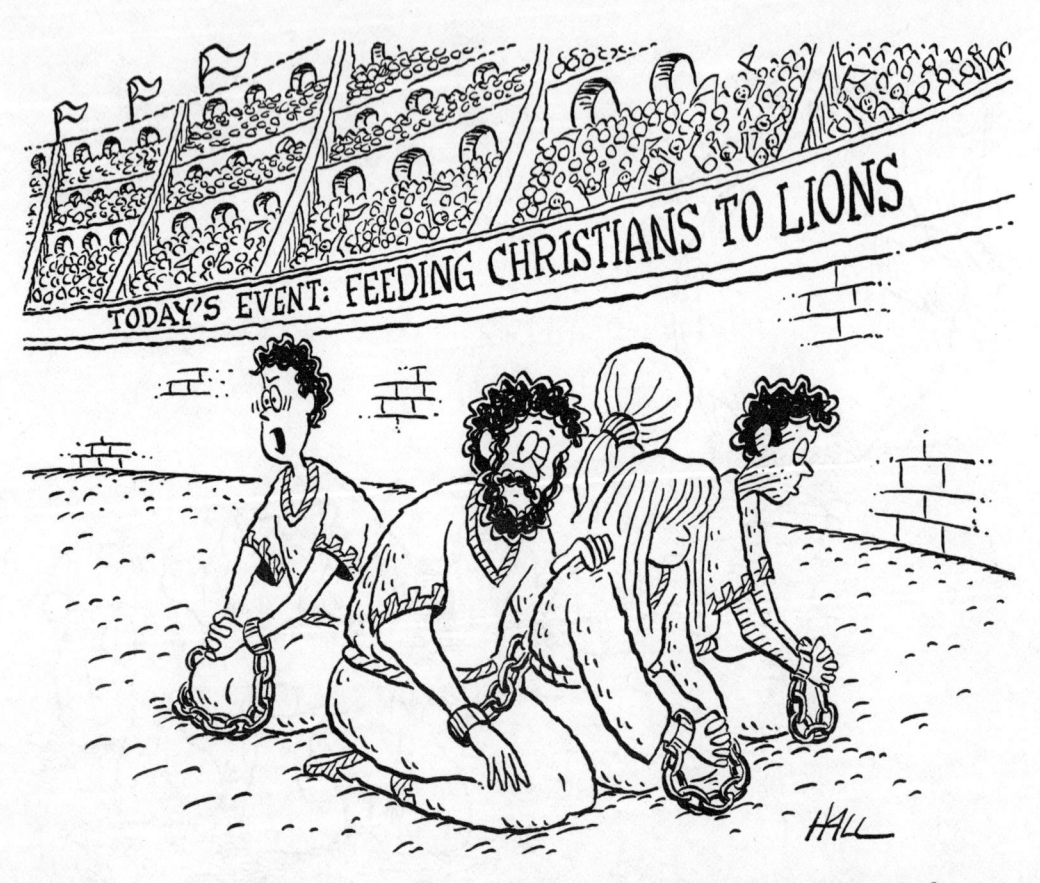

"Marcus said, 'Wanna join the youth group? We do lots of fun stuff!' And I said, 'Sure! What do I have to lose?'"

"The children are now dismissed to play 'Slay the Philistines' on our video game system."

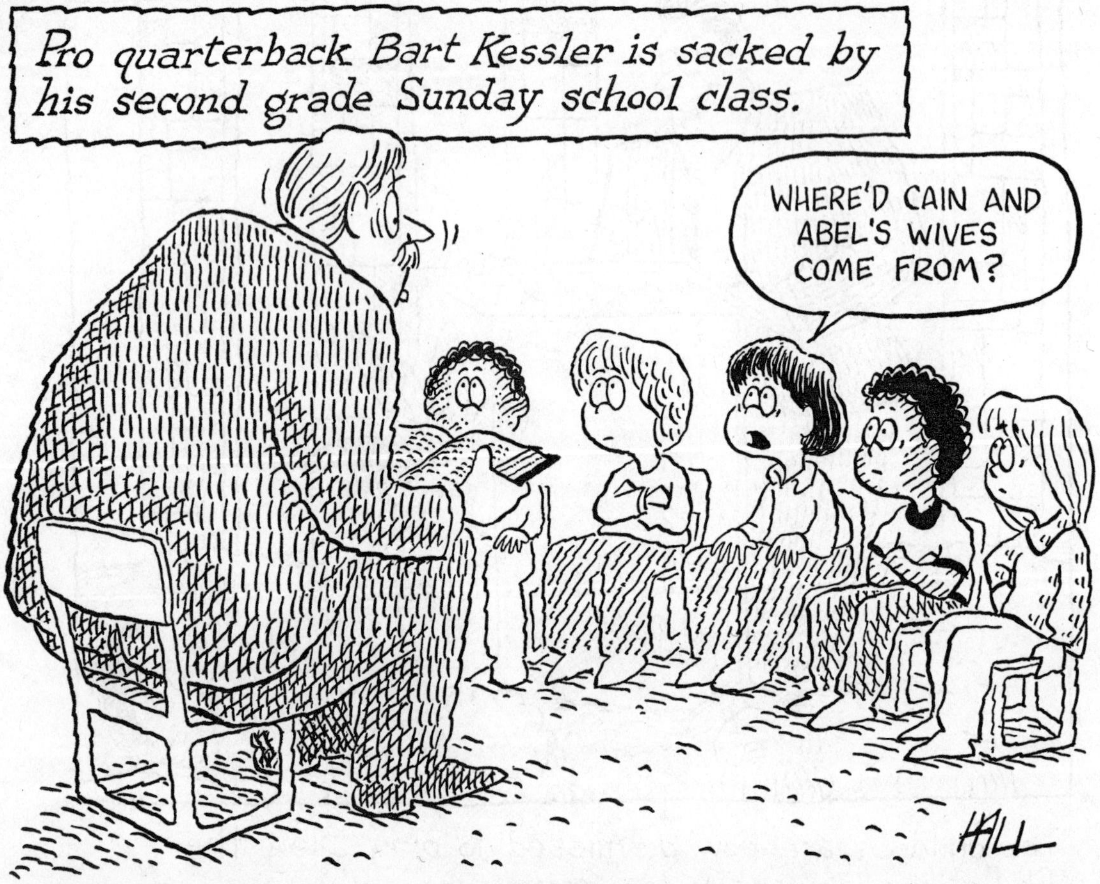
Pro quarterback Bart Kessler is sacked by his second grade Sunday school class.
WHERE'D CAIN AND ABEL'S WIVES COME FROM?
HALL

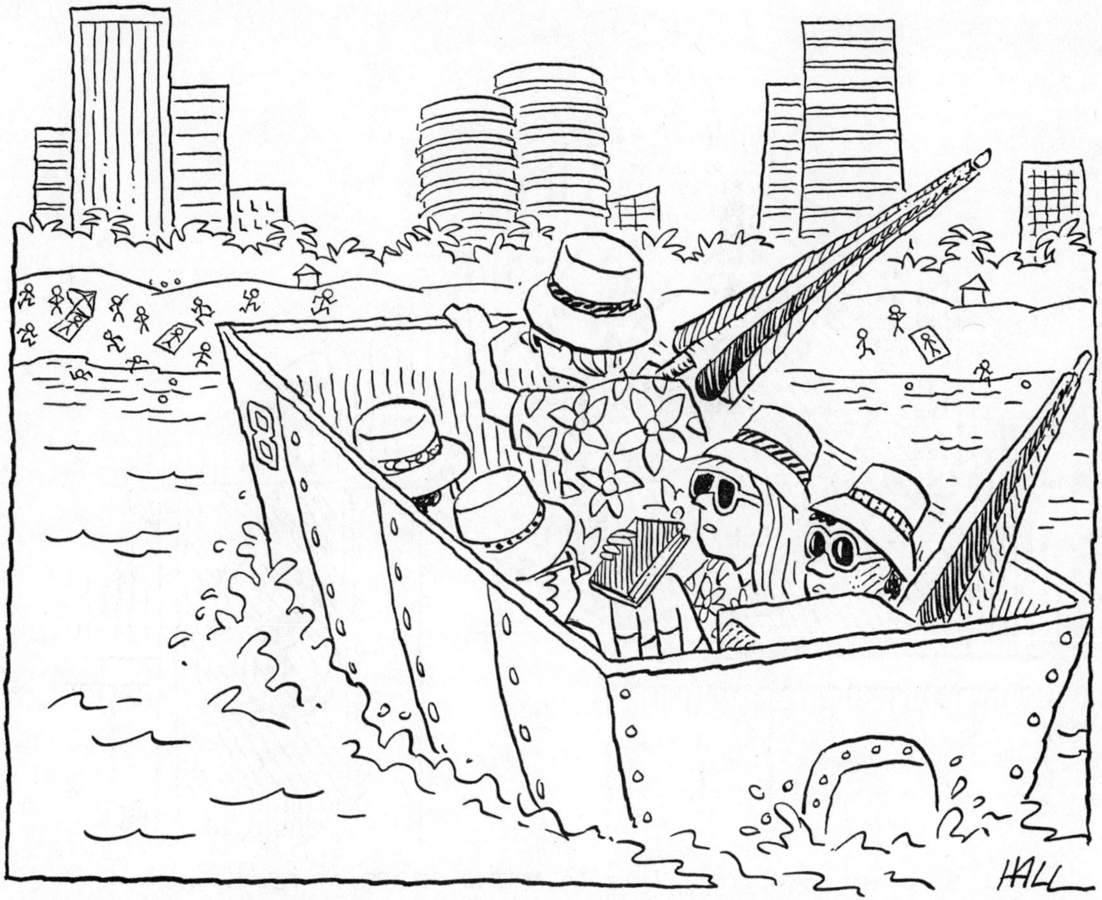
8
HALL

The Amphibious Evangelism Squad prepares to hit the beach.

"I've stopped expecting you to make leaps of faith, but it would be nice to see a hop now and then."

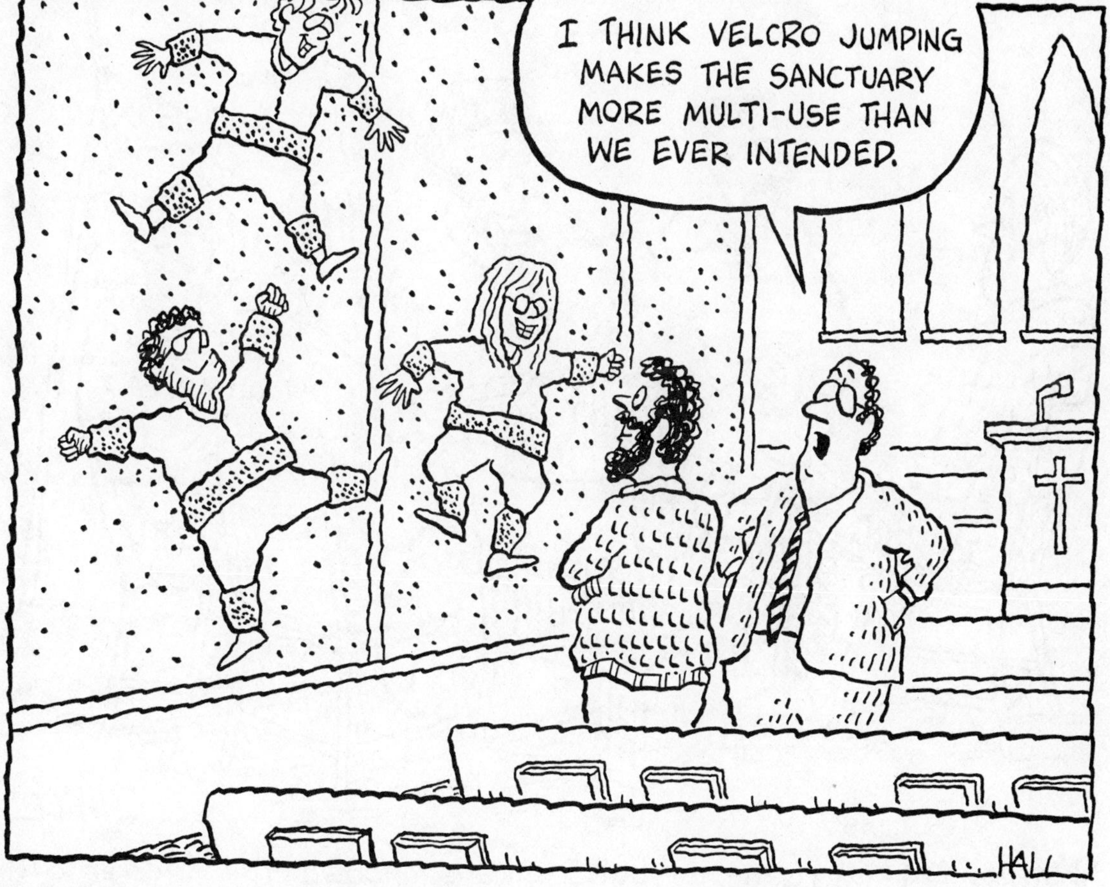
I THINK VELCRO JUMPING MAKES THE SANCTUARY MORE MULTI-USE THAN WE EVER INTENDED.
HALL

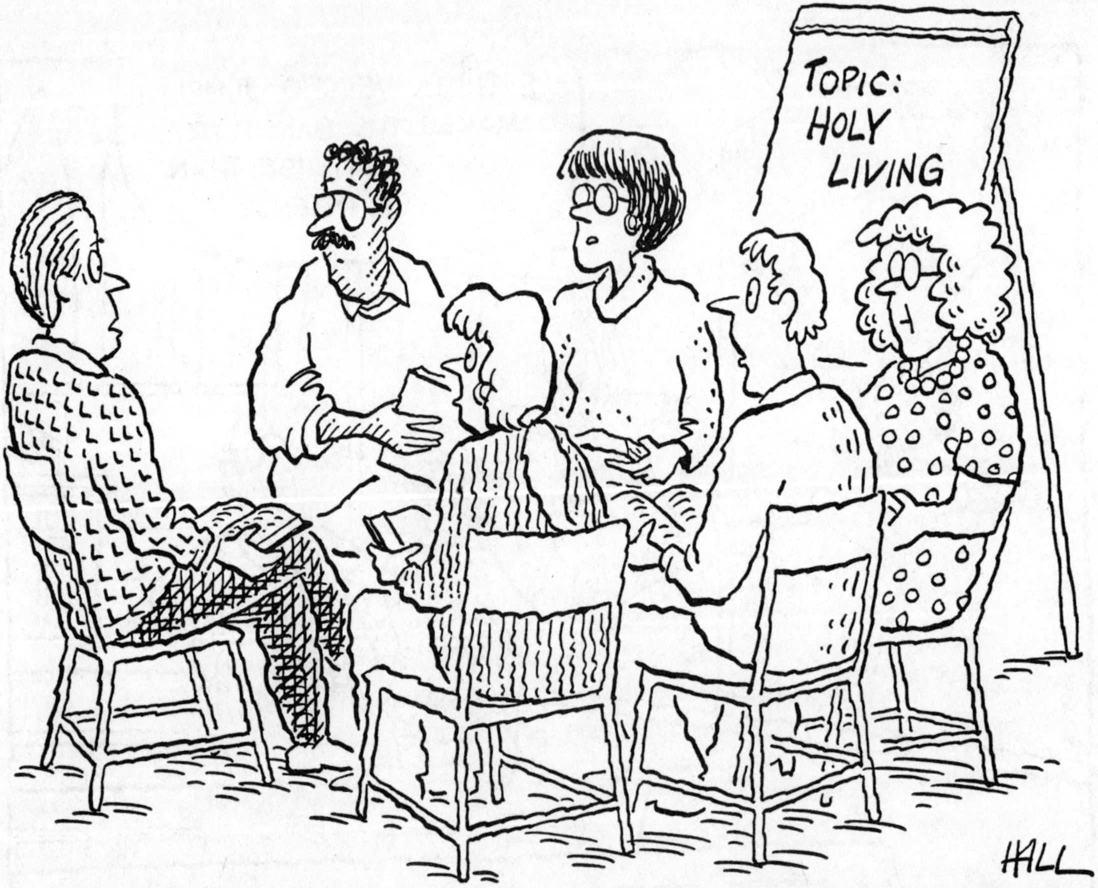
TOPIC:
HOLY
LIVING
HALL

"I'm not exactly righteous, but I always choose the lesser of two evils."

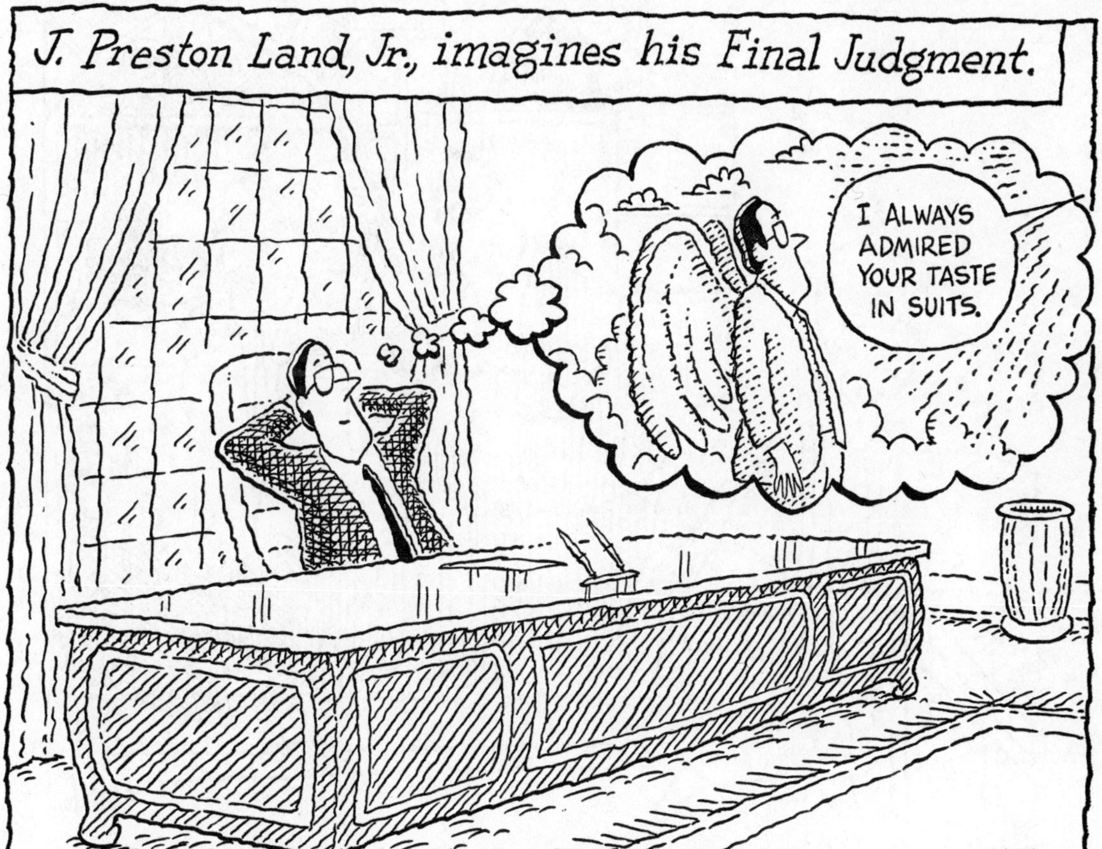
J. Preston Land, Jr., imagines his Final Judgment.
I ALWAYS ADMIRED YOUR TASTE IN SUITS.
HALL

"On the other hand, Pastor, I appreciate your willingness to tackle controversial issues."

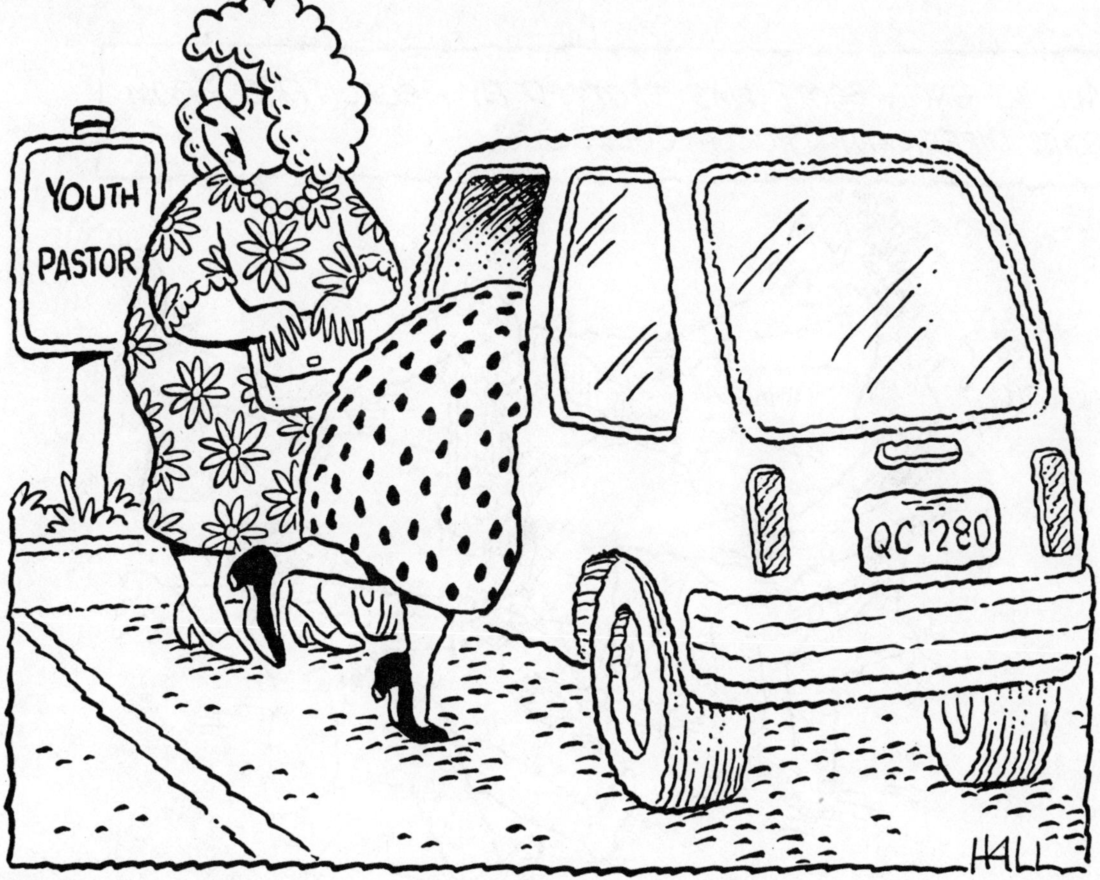
YOUTH
PASTOR
QC 1280
HALL

"Quick, Henrietta! Find out what stations her radio buttons are set to!"

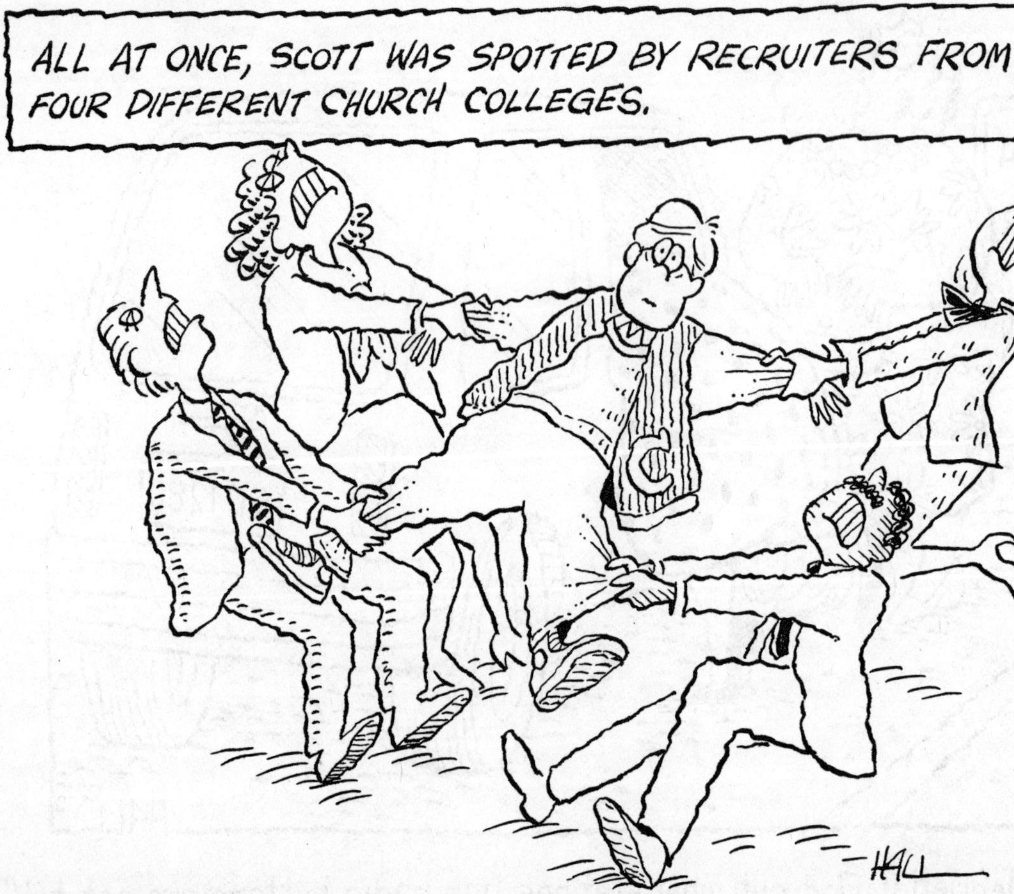
ALL AT ONCE, SCOTT WAS SPOTTED BY RECRUITERS FROM FOUR DIFFERENT CHURCH COLLEGES.
HALL

"...And if our theology doesn't grab you, our denomination offers an affinity credit card with an 11.6% annual rate."

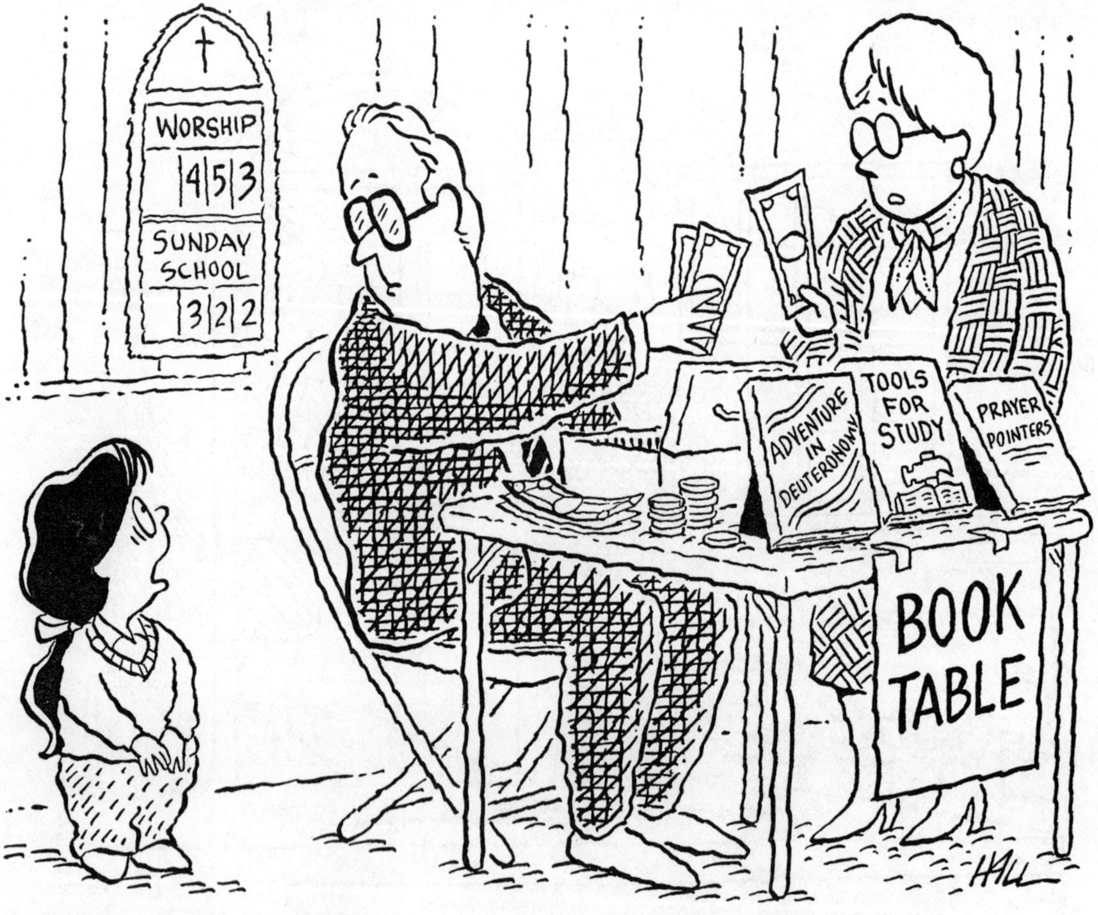
WORSHIP
453
SUNDAY SCHOOL
322
ADVENTURE IN DEUTERONOMY
TOOLS FOR STUDY
PRAYER POINTERS
BOOK TABLE
HALL

"Didn't Jesus drive all you people out of the Temple?"

"Welcome to Elm Bluff Church. The Pastor needs encouragement, so we hope you'll respond to his altar call."

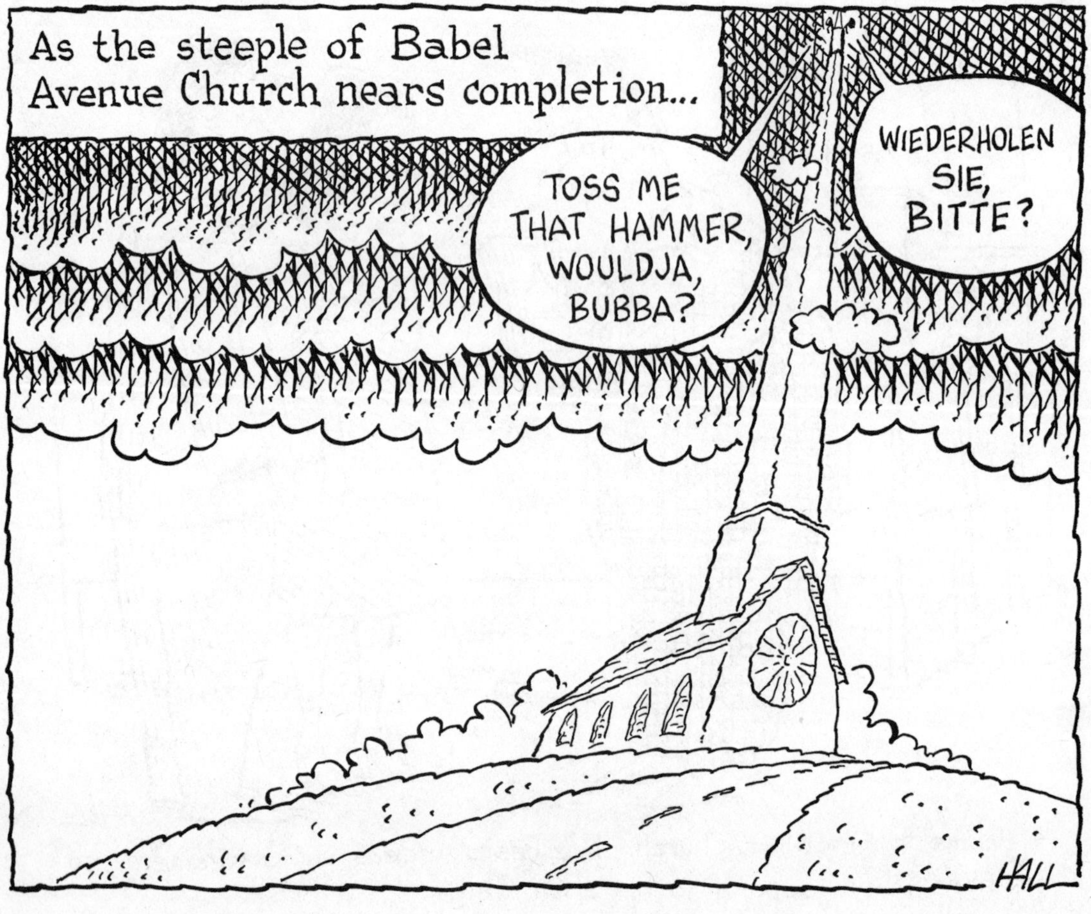
As the steeple of Babel Avenue Church nears completion...
TOSS ME THAT HAMMER, WOULDJA, BUBBA?
WIEDERHOLEN SIE, BITTE?
HALL

SMALL
GROUPS
FORMING
NOW
HALL

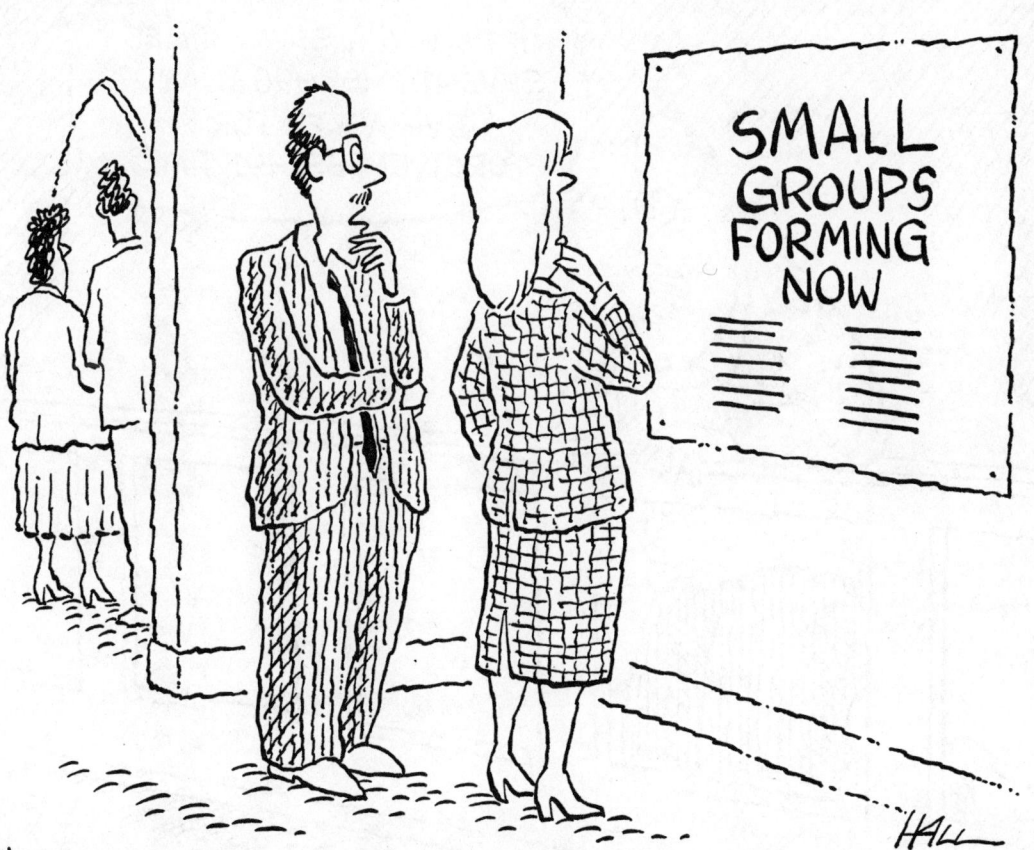

"I won't commit to any group that doesn't have a mission statement, written bylaws, and its own T-shirt."

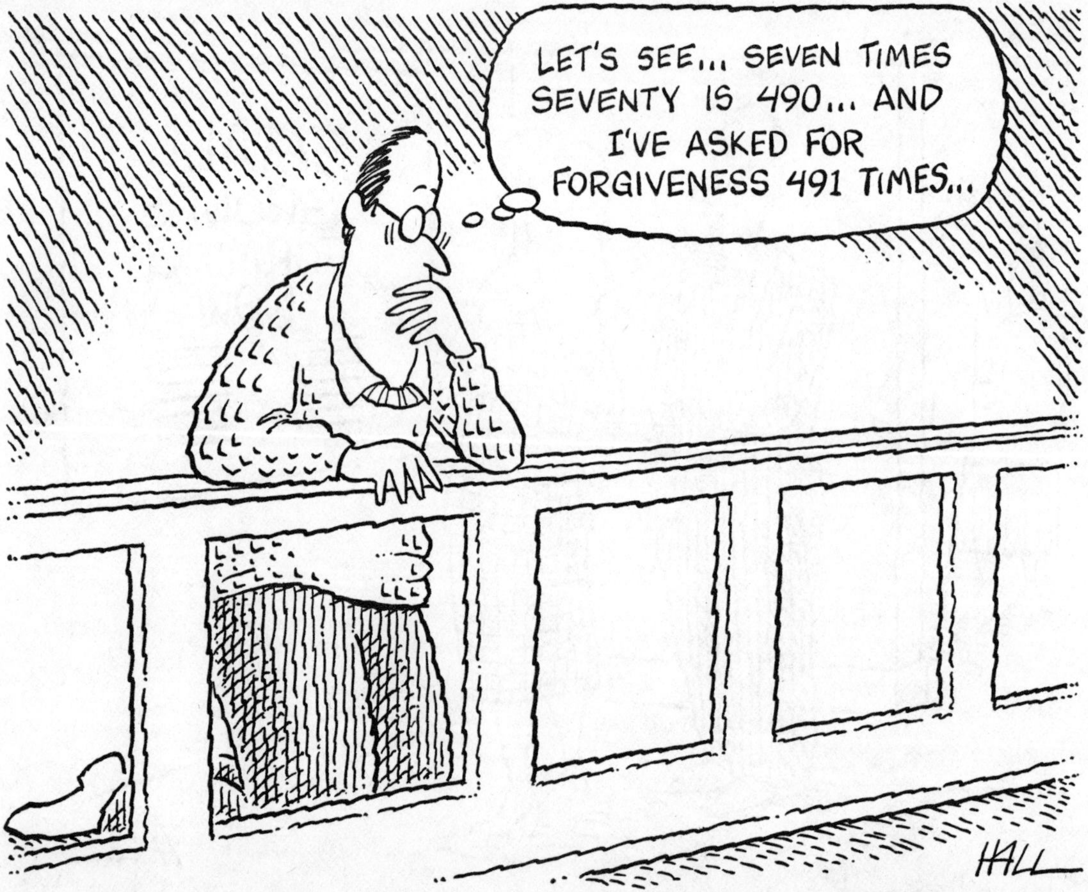
LET'S SEE... SEVEN TIMES SEVENTY IS 490... AND I'VE ASKED FOR FORGIVENESS 491 TIMES...
HALL

The day Harold Nessman stopped being a legalist.

FIRST CHURCH 7
FIRST CHURCH 8
HALL

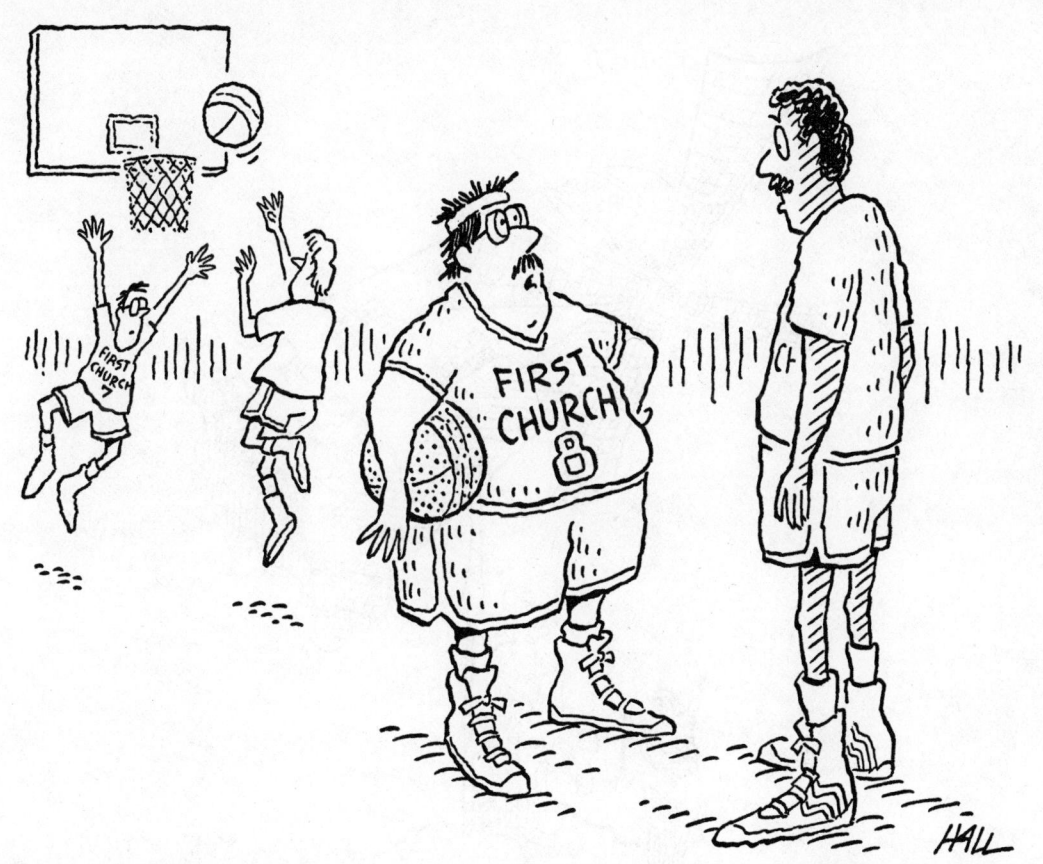

"I don't have time to be a youth counselor. The Lord wants me to work on my skyhook."

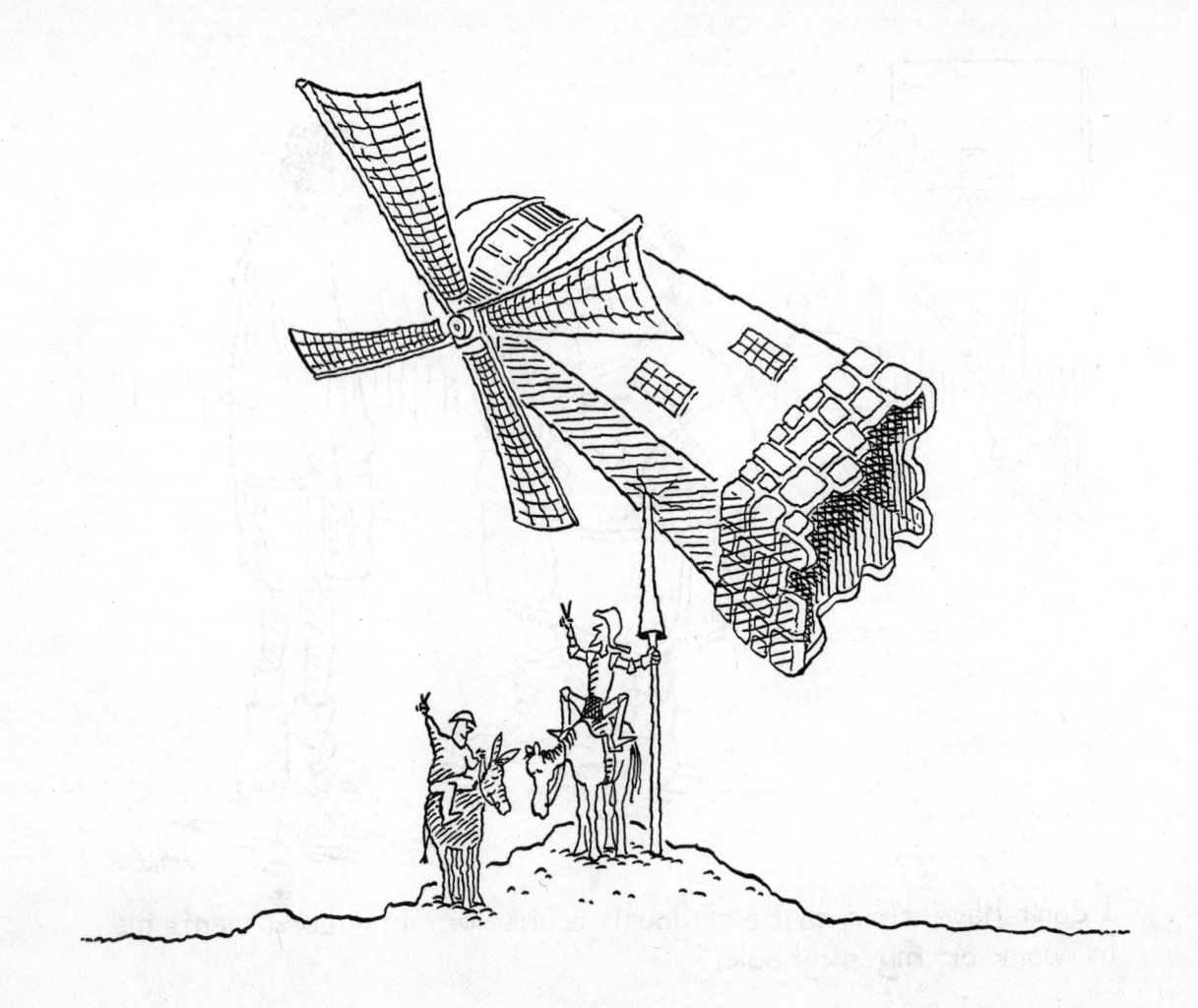

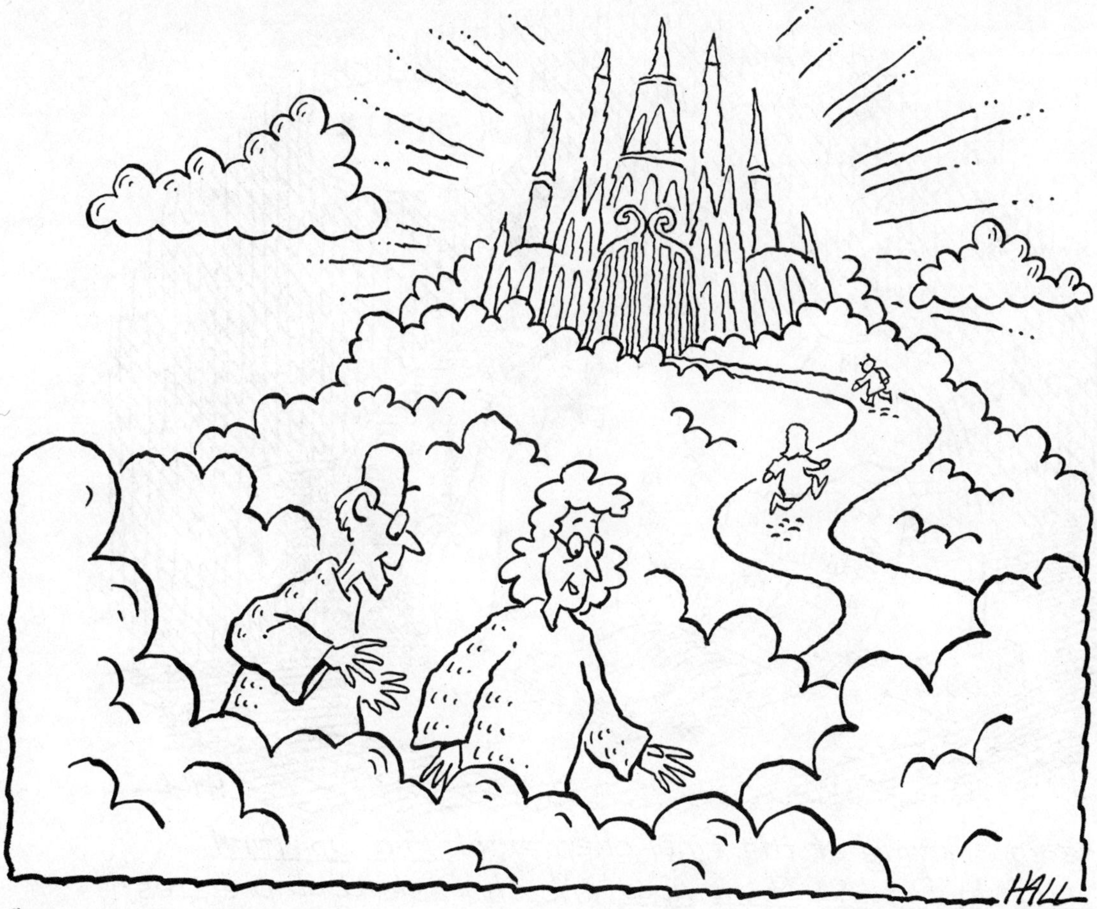
HALL

"Hey, look! The road to heaven is paved with good intentions too."

Again arriving at the final chapter of <u>Fun Spiritual Stuff to Do and Think About</u>, Youth Pastor Bob prepares to move on to yet another church.

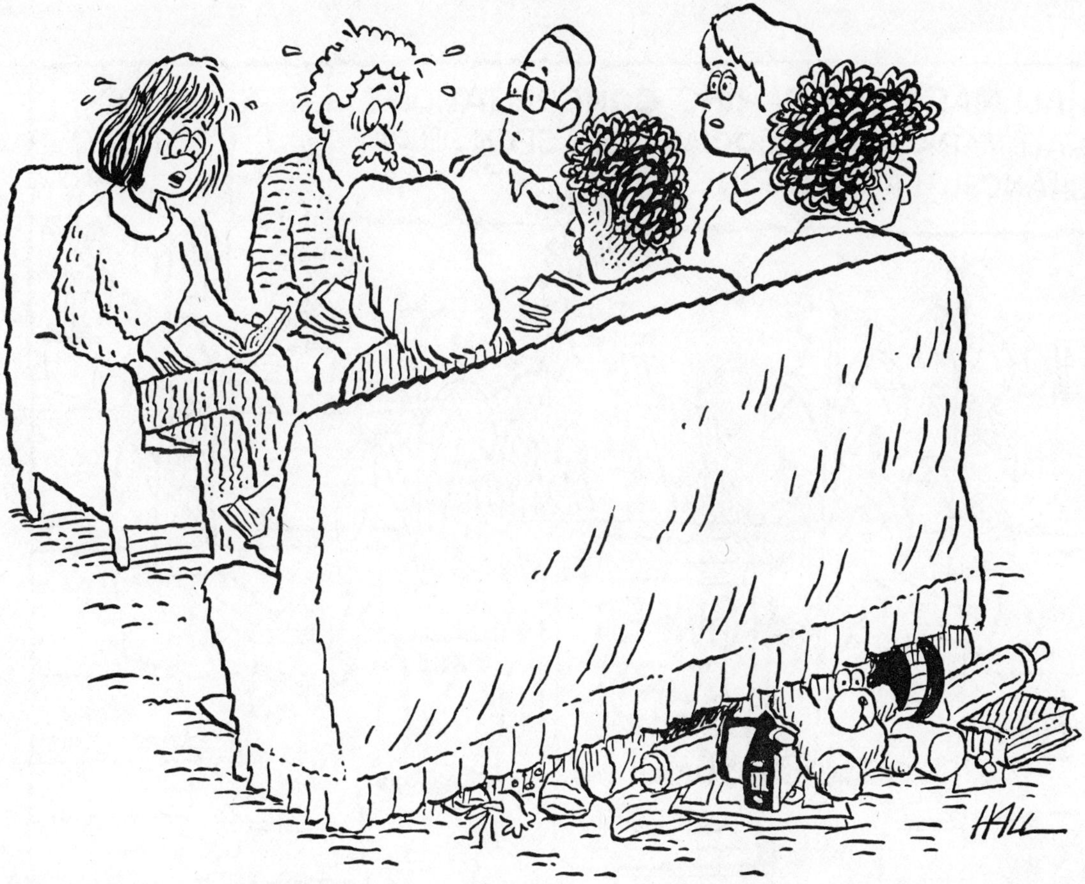
HALL

"The biggest challenge of leading a home group is cleaning the house."

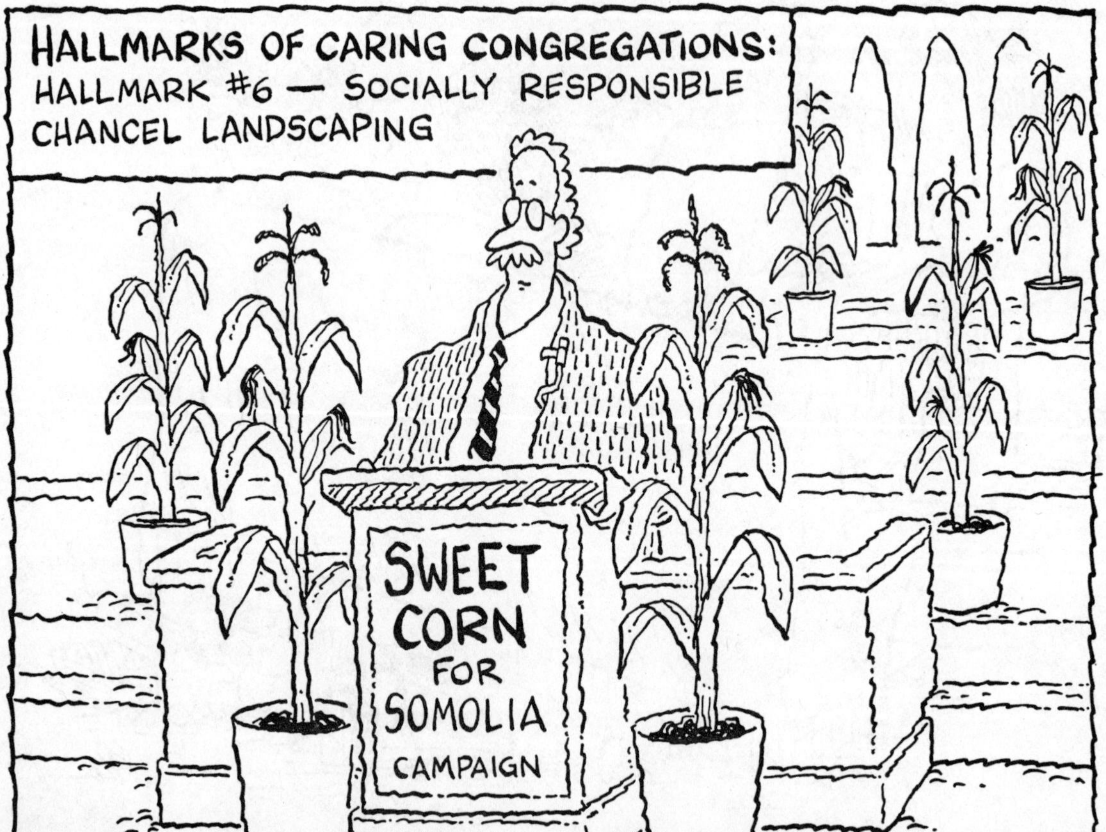
HALLMARKS OF CARING CONGREGATIONS:
HALLMARK #6 — SOCIALLY RESPONSIBLE CHANCEL LANDSCAPING
SWEET CORN FOR SOMOLIA CAMPAIGN
HALL

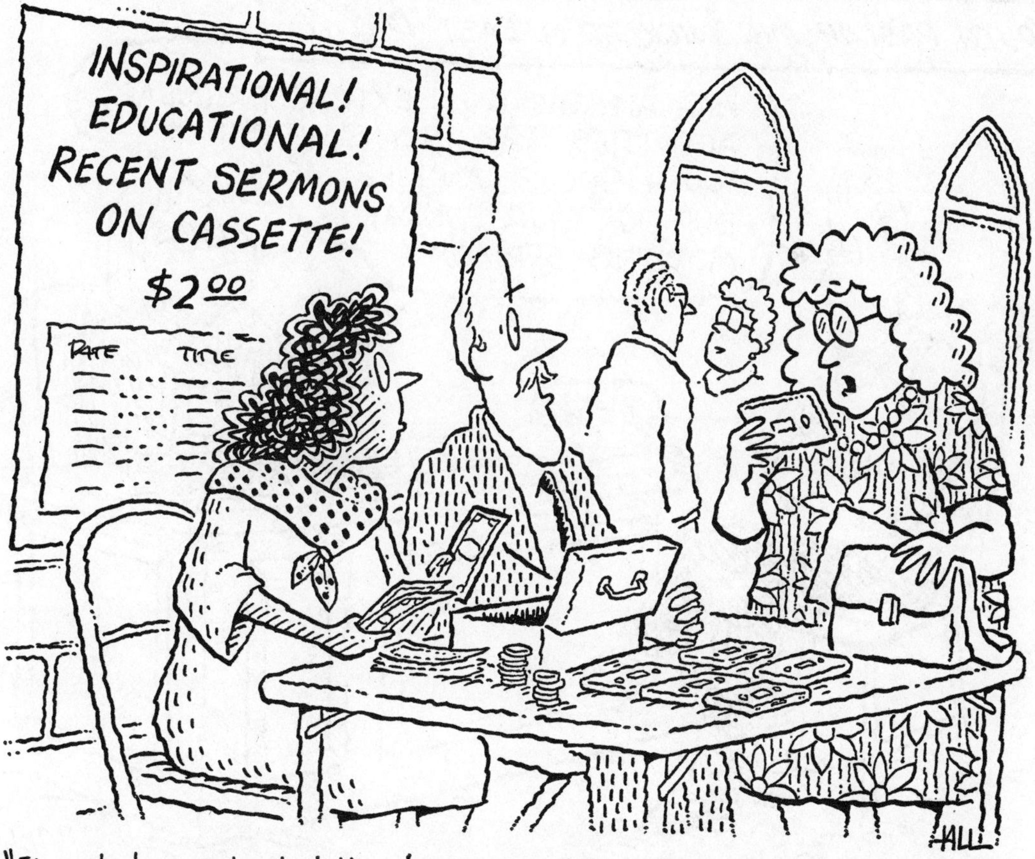
INSPIRATIONAL!
EDUCATIONAL!
RECENT SERMONS
ON CASSETTE!
$2.00
DATE
TITLE
HALL

"I'm glad we started the tape ministry. It makes it easier to pick out the pastor's grammatical errors."

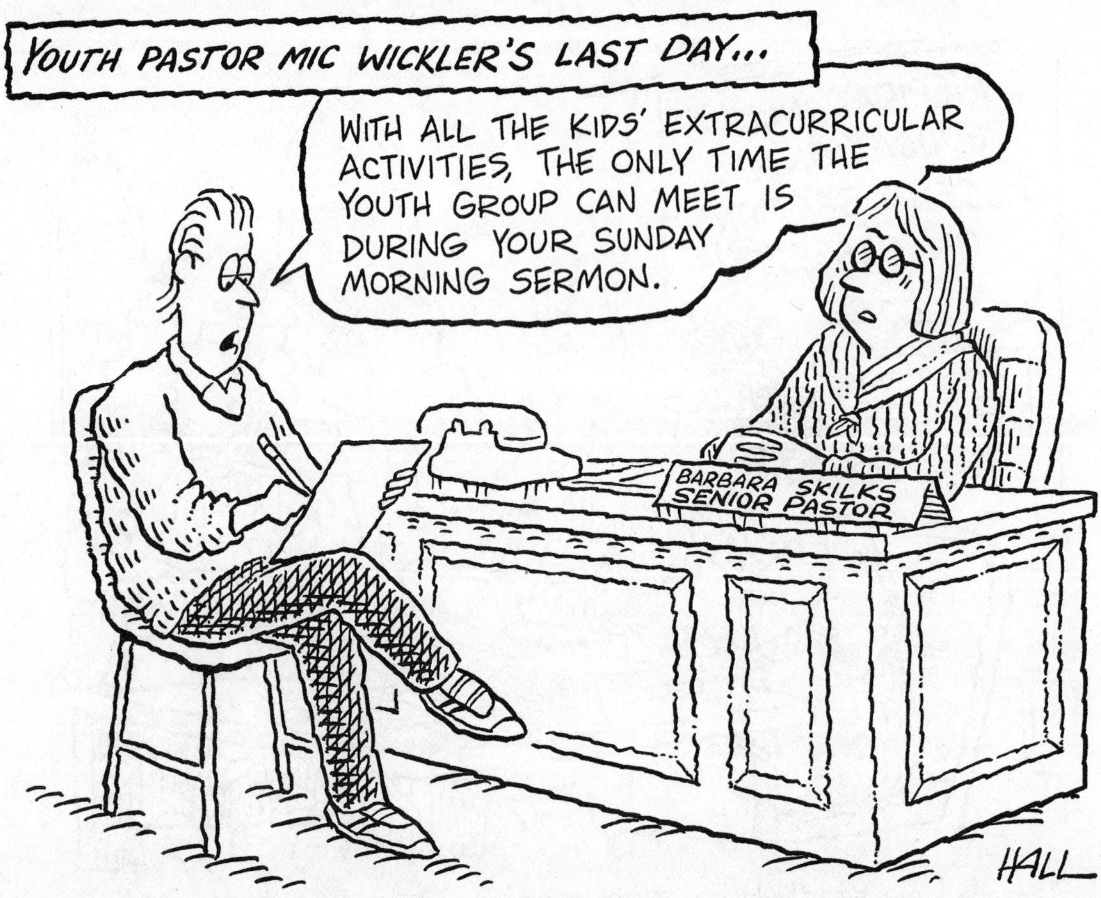
YOUTH PASTOR MIC WICKLER'S LAST DAY...
WITH ALL THE KIDS' EXTRACURRICULAR ACTIVITIES, THE ONLY TIME THE YOUTH GROUP CAN MEET IS DURING YOUR SUNDAY MORNING SERMON.
BARBARA SKILKS SENIOR PASTOR
HALL

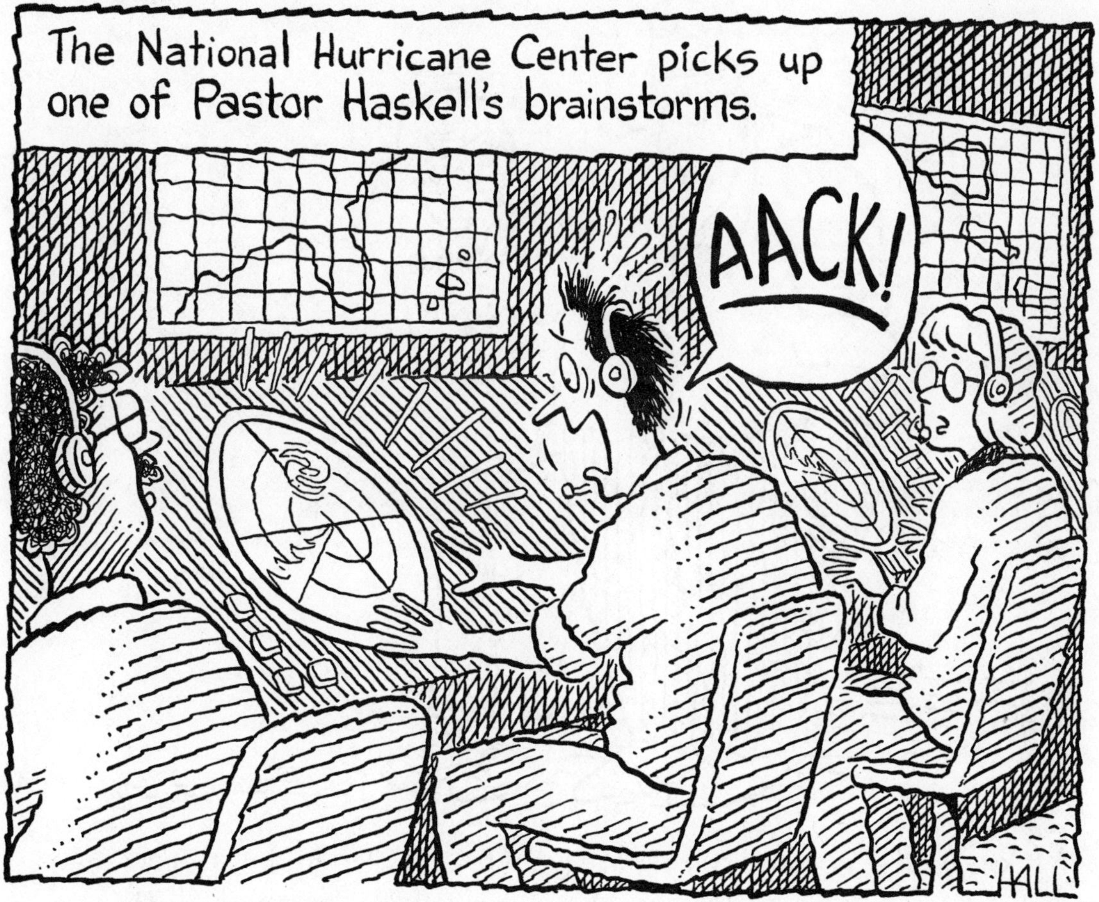
The National Hurricane Center picks up one of Pastor Haskell's brainstorms.
AACK!
HALL

"I know life is more complicated now, Son. When I was your age, all my problems could have been solved by a good acne medication."

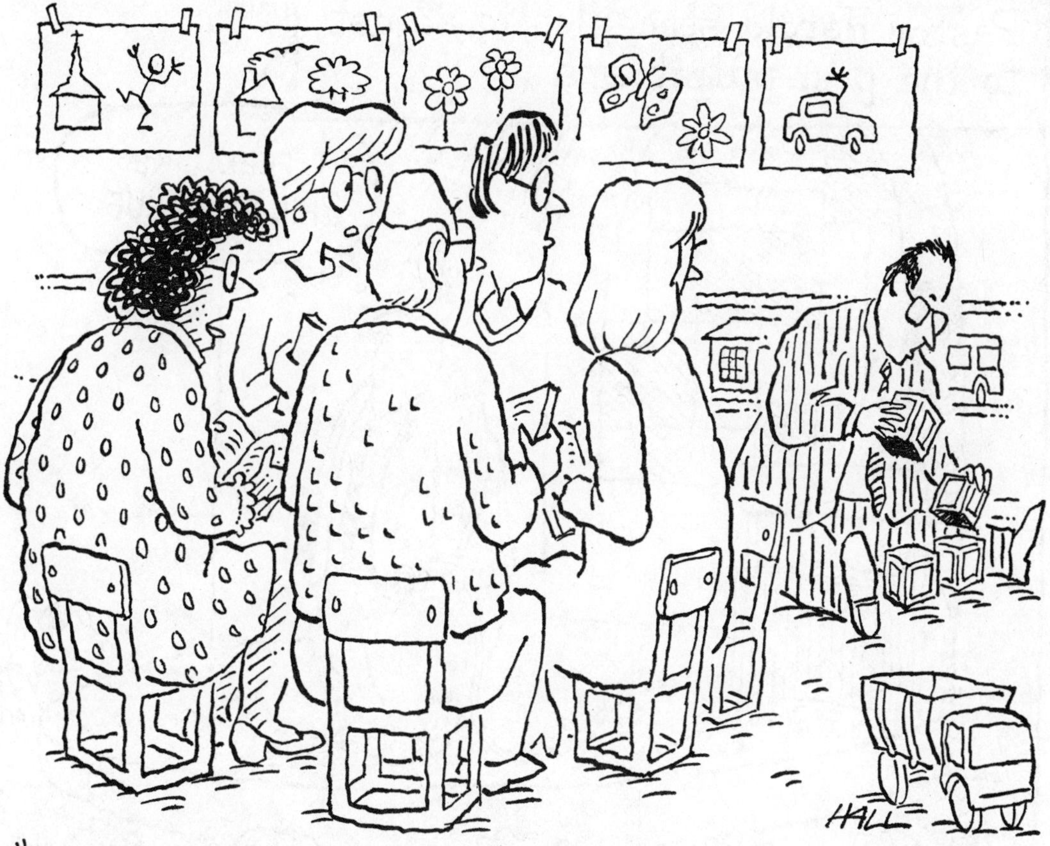
HALL

"Our group needs a new meeting room. We can't keep Earl away from the blocks."

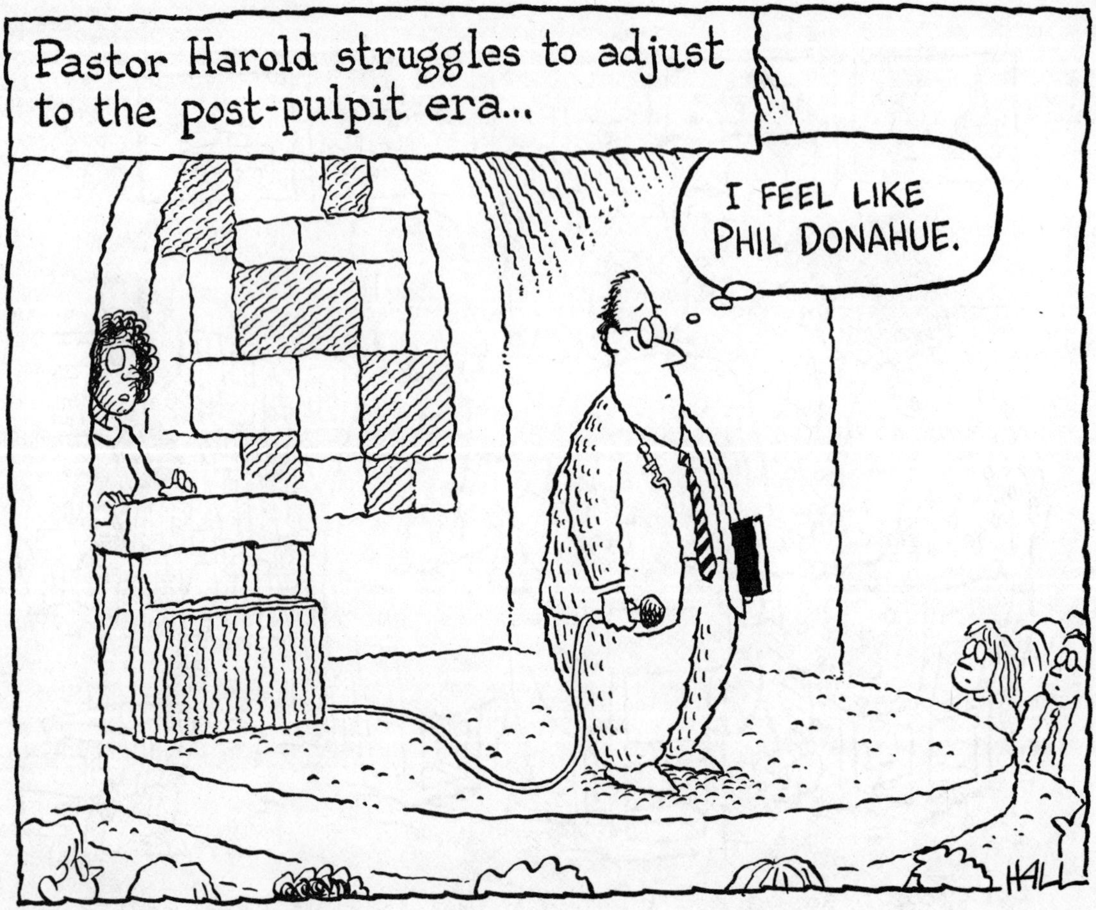
Pastor Harold struggles to adjust to the post-pulpit era...
I FEEL LIKE PHIL DONAHUE.
HALL

DENOMINATIONAL
HYMNAL
COMMITTEE
?
HALL

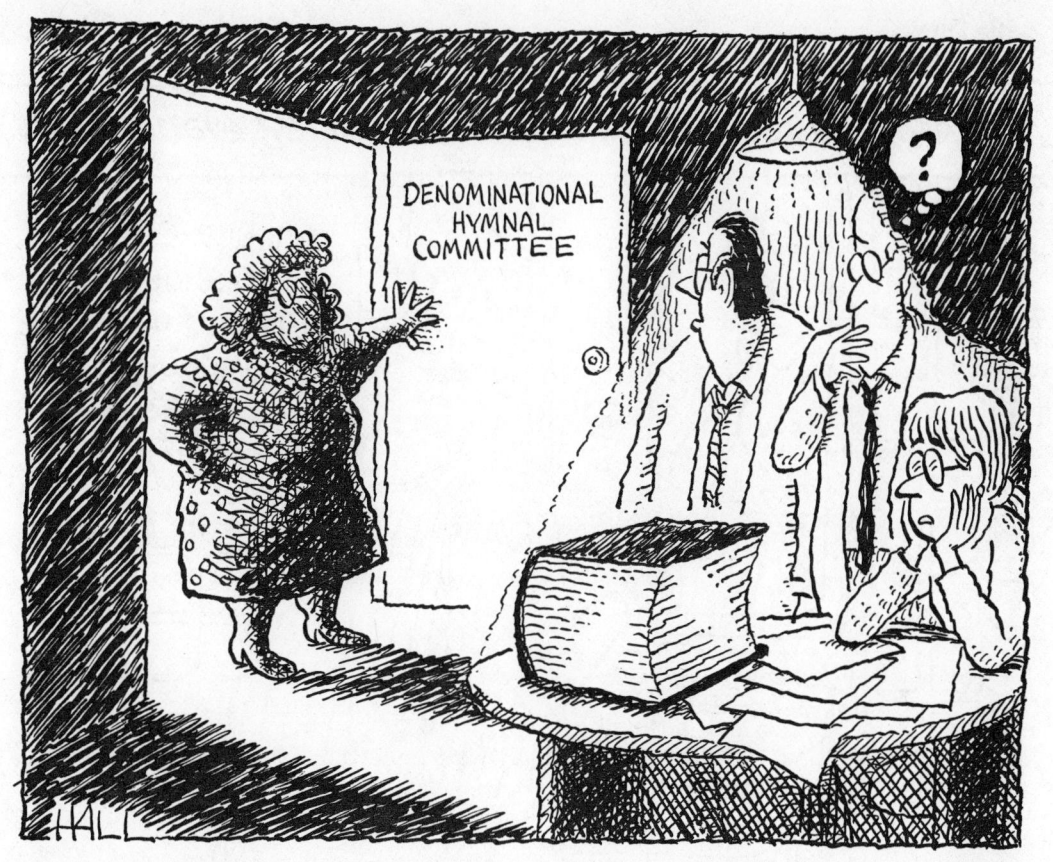

Then she appeared — the woman with enough guts to cut old favorites and get the new hymnal down to pew weight.

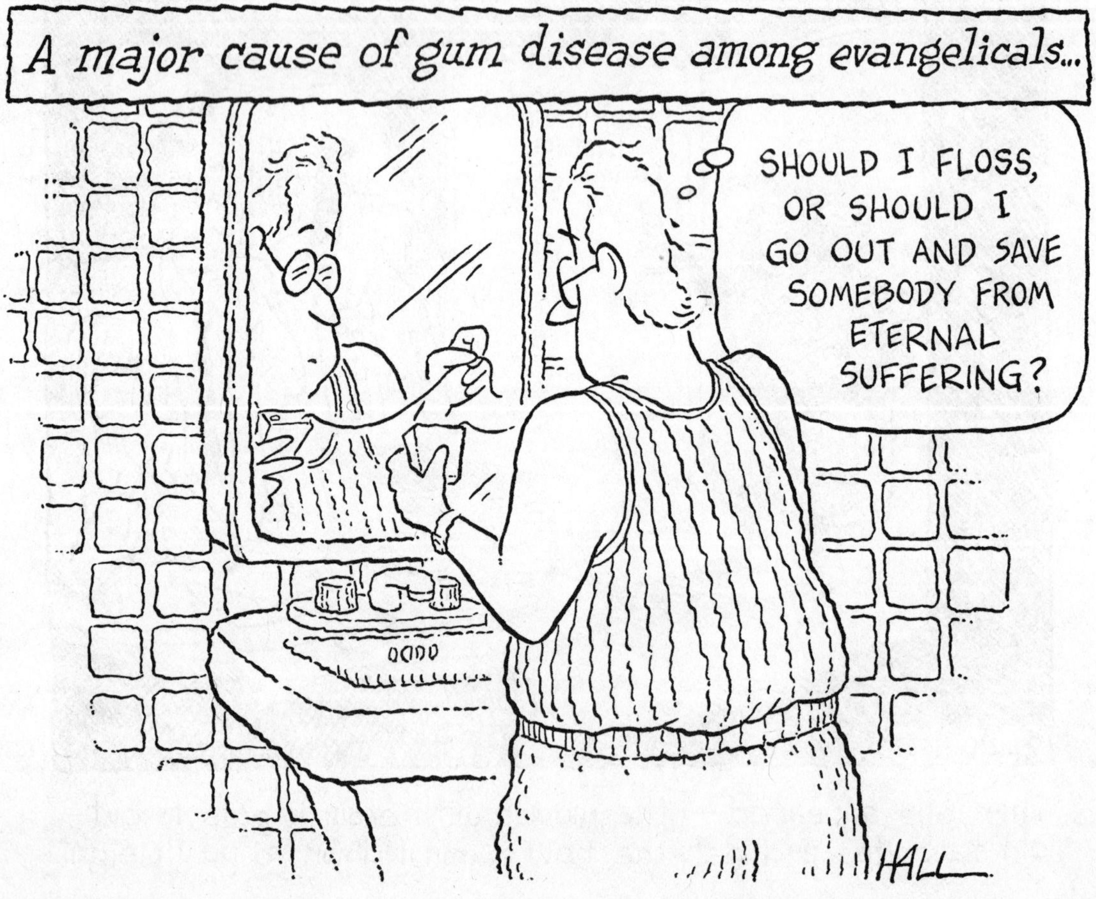
A major cause of gum disease among evangelicals...
SHOULD I FLOSS, OR SHOULD I GO OUT AND SAVE SOMEBODY FROM ETERNAL SUFFERING?
HALL

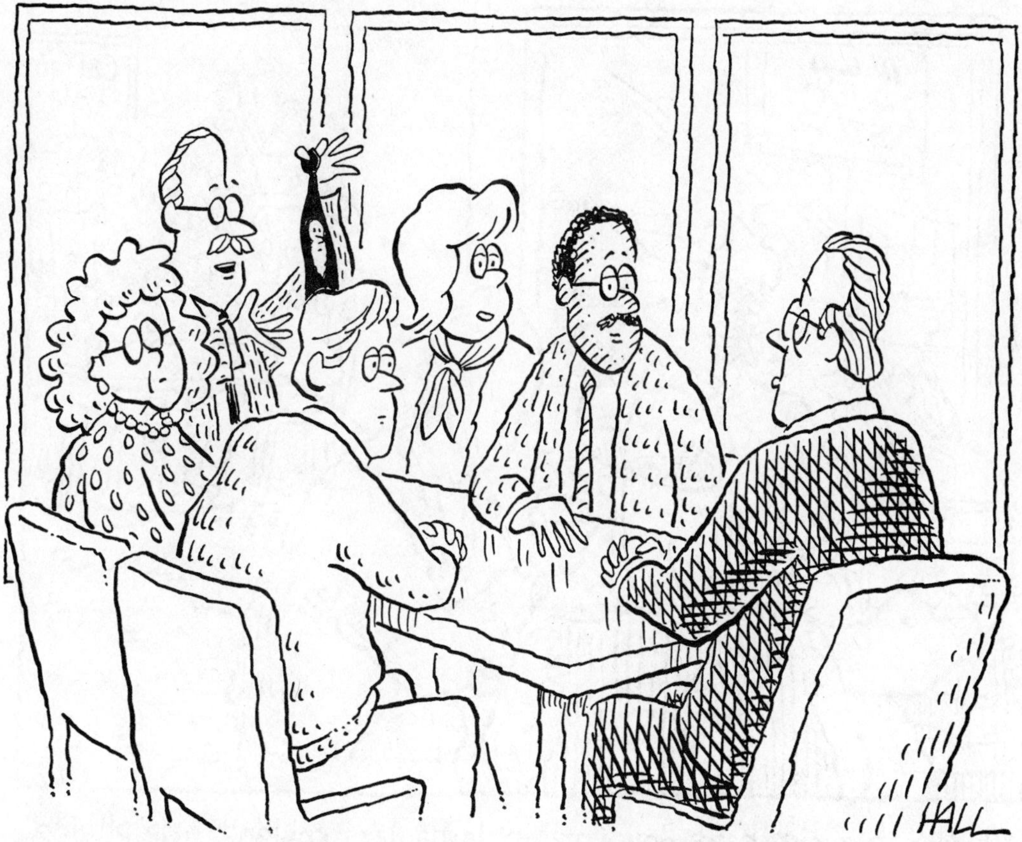
HALL

"Pastor, we've invested your pension fund in hand-painted neckties featuring the minor prophets."

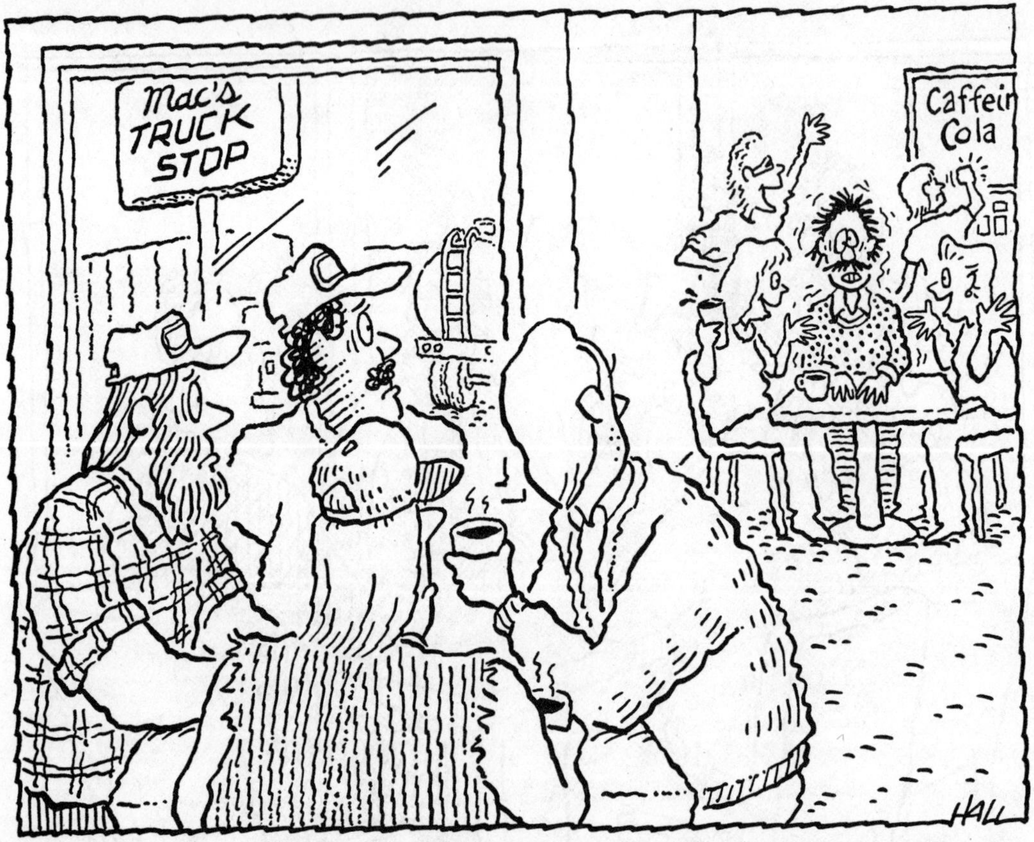
Mac's
TRUCK
STOP
Caffein
Cola
HALL

All the big-rig hazardous materials haulers couldn't help pitying the bus driver with the unstable load of seventh graders.

MAPLE
STREET
CHURCH
HALL

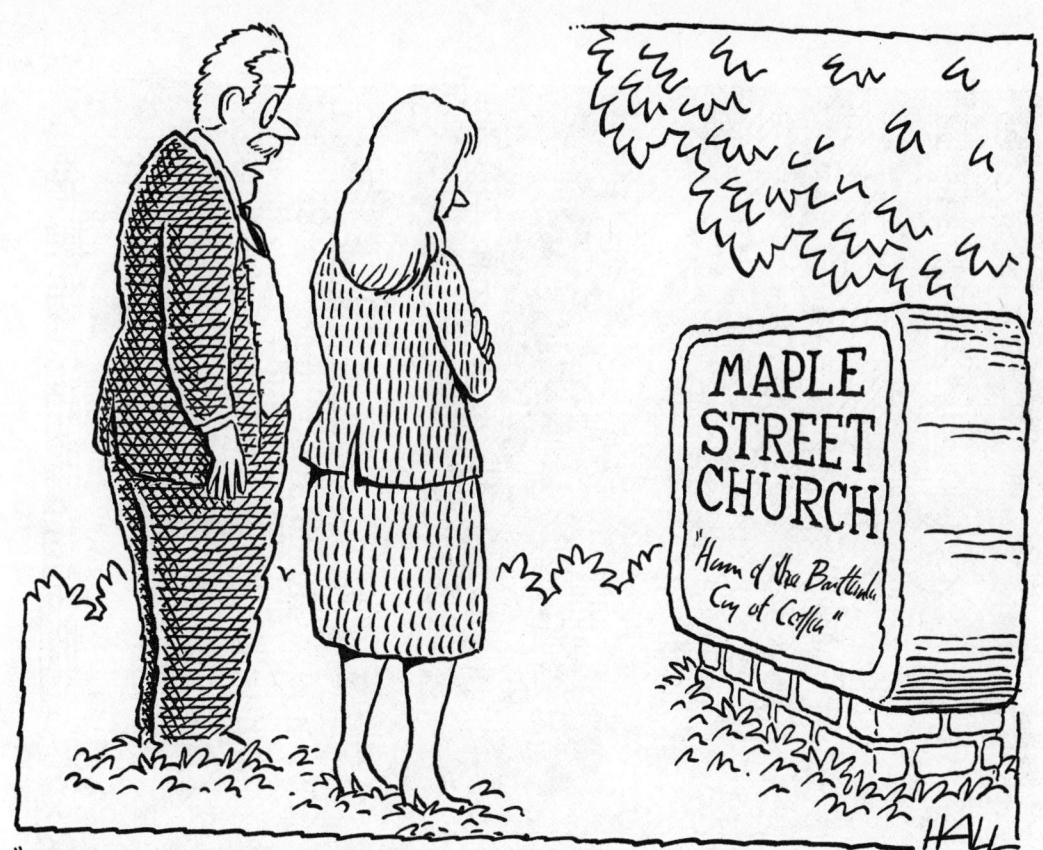

"Regardless of attendance figures, I thought 'A Community of Christian Love' was a better slogan than 'Home of the Bottomless Cup of Coffee.'"

"I have accepted a call to be on-board chaplain for Confetti Cruise Lines, 'The Perky Ships That Go to All the Perky Places.'"

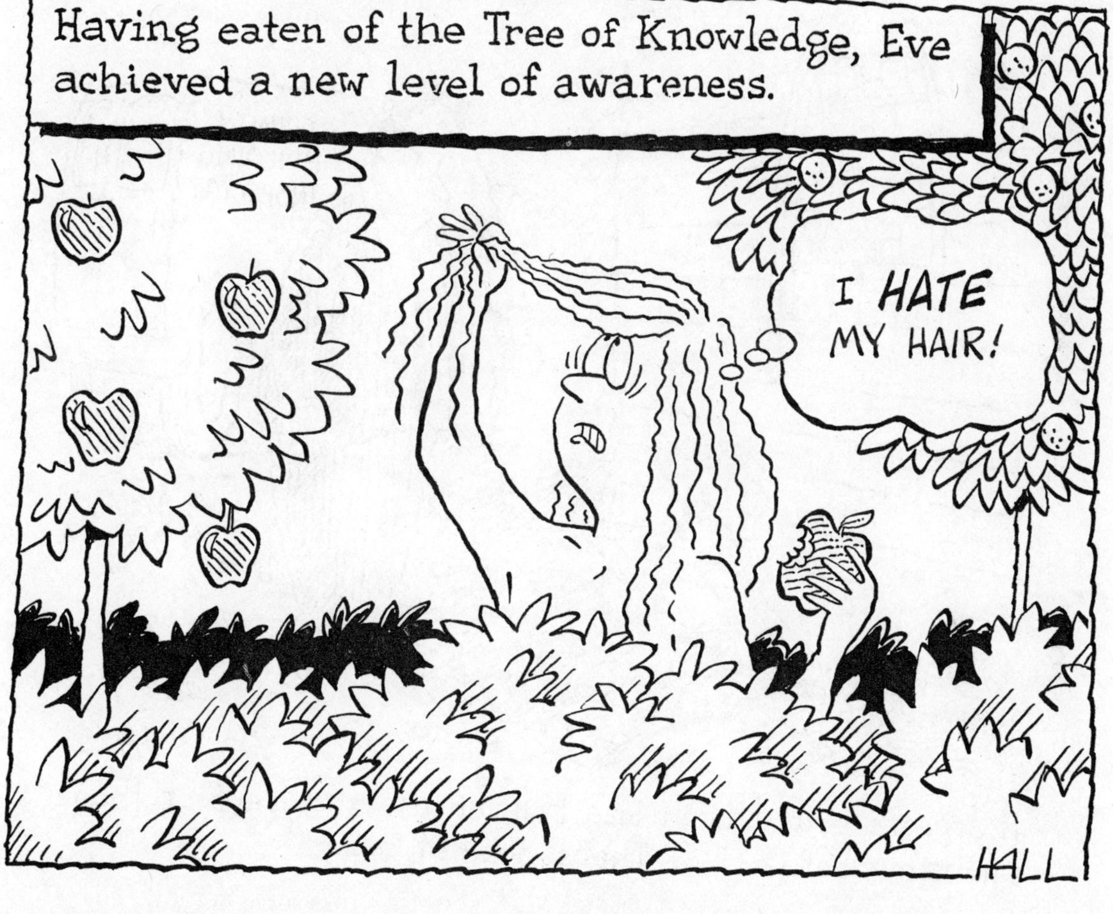
Having eaten of the Tree of Knowledge, Eve achieved a new level of awareness.
I HATE MY HAIR!
HALL

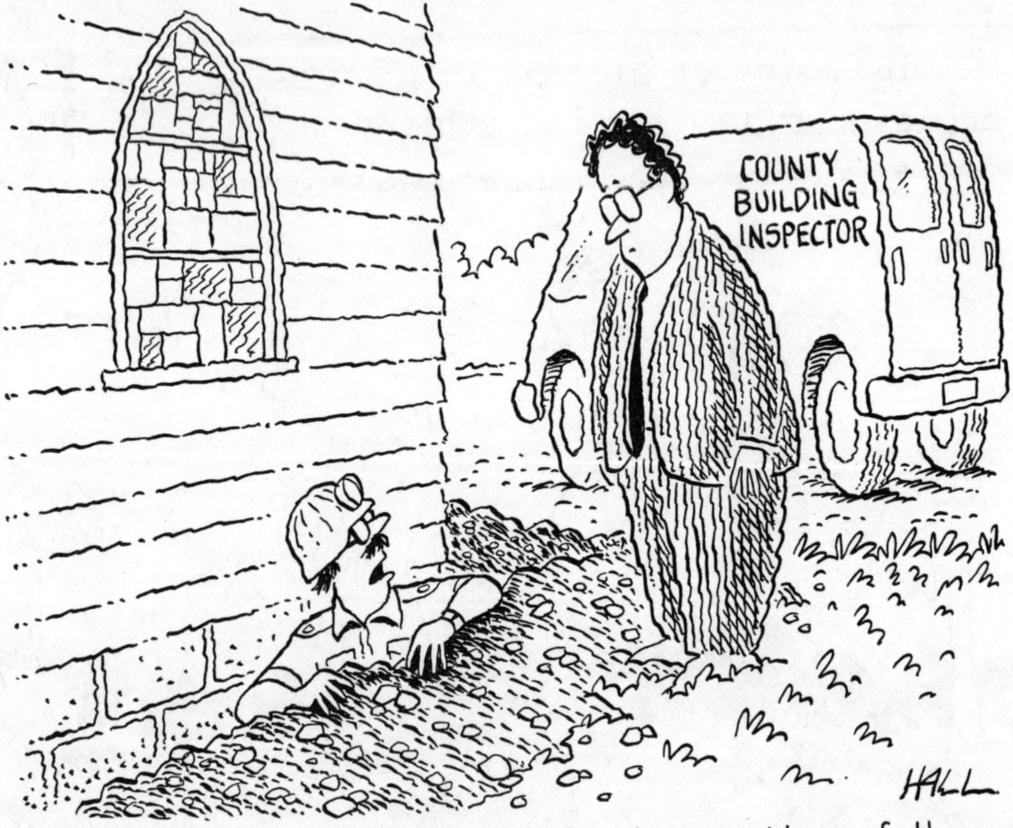

"It appears your church was built on the shoulders of those who came before you. That's against code."